# Security and Site Design

# Security and Site Design

A Landscape Architectural Approach to Analysis, Assessment, and Design Implementation

Leonard J. Hopper

Martha J. Droge

WILEY

JOHN WILEY & SONS, INC.

Published by John Wiley & Sons, Inc., Hoboken, New Jersey
Published simultaneously in Canada

For general information on our other products and services or for technical support, please contact our Customer Care Department within the United States at 800-762-2974, outside the United States at (317) 572-3993 or fax (317) 572-4002.

Wiley also publishes its books in a variety of electronic formats. Some content that appears in print may not be available in electronic books.

*Library of Congress Cataloging-in-Publication Data:*

Hopper, Leonard J.
  Security and site design : a landscape architectural approach to analysis, assessment, and design implementation / Leonard J. Hopper, Martha J. Droge.
        p. cm.
  Includes bibliographical references.
  ISBN 0-471-65583-X (cloth : alk. paper)
1.  Building sites--United States--Planning. 2.  Public buildings--Security measures--United States. 3.  Terrorism--United States--Prevention. 4.  Landscape architecture.  I. Droge, Martha J. II. Title.
  NA2540.5.H67 2005
  711'.1--dc22

                                                                2004025689

Printed in the United States of America

10 9 8 7 6 5 4 3 2 1

*Len dedicates this book to his loving wife Cindy
and all their children, who make everything
so worthwhile.*

*Martha dedicates this book to her parents for their
love, support, and encouragement.*

# Contents

vii

CHAPTER **3**    **Site Security Design Concepts** . . . . . **33**

CHAPTER **4**    **Case Studies** . . . . . . . . . . . . . . . . . . . . **77**

# Acknowledgments

The authors appreciate the support and assistance of the many people who participated in the creation of *Security and Site Design*.

We would like to particularly acknowledge the generosity of the National Capital Planning Commission for allowing the reprint of text and images from the *National Capital Urban Design and Security Plan*, with special thanks for help from Patricia E. Gallagher, AICP, Executive Director, Elizabeth Miller, ASLA, Lisa N. MacSpadden, Stephen Staudigl, and Paul Jutton.

The General Services Administration (GSA) very generously gave permission to present informative images and text. Our thanks go to Frank V. Giblin, AICP, Urban Development/Good Neighbor Program in the Office of the Chief Architect at GSA. We are also grateful to Todd Bressi, author of *Before the Jersey Barrier: Public Access and Public Safety in Federal Buildings*, which describes the Hanley Federal Building and U.S. Courthouse, Syracuse, New York, for permission to reprint his work.

We thank The American Institute of Architects, which graciously allowed us to reproduce material from their highly regarded publication, *Security Planning and Design: A Guide for Architects and Building Design Professionals*.

We also thank John Nicolaus, ASLA, Scott Redding, ASLA, and the HLA Group for sharing their innovative security design approach and site elements for the California State House in Sacramento, as well as George Vellonakis for sharing his insight and stories, which provided such wonderful background into the process and design of the revitalized government center of New York City, City Hall Park.

Finally, we extend our gratitude to John Wiley & Sons, Inc., and in particular Margaret Cummins, Senior Editor; Rosanne Koneval, Senior Editorial Assistant; and Donna Conte, Senior Production Editor, for their guidance and support throughout the project.

A Complimentary review copy from

WILEY

*Publishers Since 1807*

Title:      SECURITY AND SITE

Author:     HOPPER

Pub Date:   04/01/05

Paper Price: 0          Paper ISBN:

Cloth Price:  65        Cloth ISBN:  047165583X

Contact:    EVELYN      201-748-6358

201-748-6395

No review should appear before publication date and Wiley would appreciate two copies of your review 111 River Street, 4th floor, Hoboken, NJ 07030

# Security Site Design

## HISTORY

Designers throughout history have included protection and security as part of their work. This included protection against the elements as well as security against those that would do them harm. Early on, site selection considered geographic features like rivers, mountains, canyons, and other natural barriers to enhance security. Security design thinking evolved into building man-made barriers like walls, fences, and moats for protection against unwanted outsiders. Such security measures were directed toward keeping intruders out, keeping them at a safe distance where they could inflict little damage, or slowing their advancement to give defenders time to respond. The physical elements of protection, natural and man-made, gave defenders a tactical edge over those seeking to do them harm.

Security design is not very different today. The primary objectives remain the same. Even the simplest of fences defines property and, however easy to circumvent, clearly shows that the trespasser is in violation of the owner's basic rights. The design of these perimeter barriers can escalate along with any associated threat. However, just about any perimeter defense can be circumvented. There will always remain some degree of risk because of physical, budget, or personnel limitations. The objective is to match an appropriate barrier with a reasonably anticipated threat.

Vigilance that is responsive to accurate assessments of actual and likely threats results in a proper level of physical and psychological precautions being taken. When threats are exaggerated or unlikely scenarios are magnified—as when, for example, broad media attention focuses on one target and overstates its importance to the general public—there can be serious repercussions. The quality of our daily lives suffers and our actions are guided by unrealistic fears. The balance between openness and the restriction of our freedom of movement, access to public buildings, and connection with our government is upset. The limited personnel and financial resources that we have to direct toward security design may be spent in ways that are less than effective and take away resources from more necessary security needs. We must exercise a rational approach to finding a balance between those that put security concerns above all others and those that argue that openness in our society must be a priority.

Finding this balance is a fundamental task in the process of security design development. The basis for a creative security design solution must be an accurate risk assessment. Security setbacks must be carefully considered for their impacts on the architectural character of the surrounding community. The elements used between the building and perimeter become critically important components in order to incorporate the security design response with the architectural context of the area. The design will provide a strong connection to the street and architectural character of the adjacent properties, as well as establish a secure perimeter. It creates a situation where those seeking to overcome the barrier look overtly obvious by the means they must carry out to break through the perimeter. Moreover, the extended time needed to defeat the perimeter security will delay would-be attackers, such that other responses can be focused on stopping them.

The range of potential threat has been broadened by scientific and technological advancement. The availability of this knowledge and accessibility of materials to carry out violent acts have added to the sophistication of the terrorist arsenal. Today, biological, radiological, and cyber terrorism have been added to the list of potential threats. These same advancements have provided enhanced security measures in our built environment to counter these new threats. The defender and terrorist are constantly engaged in the effort to be one step ahead and gain a tactical advantage.

The response to terrorist threat must be multifaceted, comprehensive, and coordinated in order to address a problem of this magnitude. Therefore, it is extremely important that the landscape architect know the anticipated threats based on thorough analysis of the threat, the site, and its context. A good security design will be based on an accurate collection of data that is responsive to the unique situations of each site rather than a prescriptive, one-size-fits-all approach that attempts to impose a predetermined design solution. Furthermore, landscape architects must actively collaborate with other professionals involved in a security design response to employ the strategies and materials available to create designs that meet the client's security and programmatic needs.

## CONTEXT IN TODAY'S SECURITY-CONSCIOUS ENVIRONMENT

"Life as we know it will never be the same after 9/11." We have heard that expression so many times, yet the impact of that day continues to affect the social, psychological, economic and physical fabric of this country and the world. As design professionals, we need to recognize and respect this change in the environment in which we live and respond to these changes in the work that we do.

The attacks on 9/11 were not without precedent, though never of the magnitude and coordination witnessed that tragic day. The attacks on U.S. embassies and facilities abroad since the 1980s were, in retrospect, preludes to 9/11 in the sense that American assets were no longer safe from foreign terrorist groups. The first bombing of the World Trade Center in New York and the bombing of the Alfred P. Murrah federal building in Oklahoma City showed that both foreign- and U.S.-born terrorists were at work in ways most Americans had not imagined.

As a coordinated effort to hijack commercial airliners unfolded, there was a lack of clear communications between those who first realized something was terribly wrong and those who would need to respond. Our air defense system, once notified, scrambled jet fighters that would not be in a position to intercept the hijacked planes but could only arrive after they had already completed their missions of destruction and death. In the hours that followed the attack, we found our emergency response systems lacked necessary coordination and redundancy to respond to an event of this magnitude. Although we paid an extraordinarily high price that day, our nation learned a great deal about threats that confront us. We recognized that mistakes were made and began instituting changes as we moved ahead into what is a very different world. As a nation, we discovered that we are not immune from the devastating terrorist strikes that we were accustomed to reading about in other parts of the world. Just as the physical design of U.S. compounds overseas responded to the need for heightened security, we now need to focus that same level of effort to safeguard our citizens and national symbols on U.S. soil.

It is now imperative that security be a critical overlay in every major public or private design project currently being considered, and existing facilities and sites must be retrofitted to enhance security. As design professionals, we are uniquely positioned to contribute to America's safety and well being, responding to the war on terror by redesigning our domestic battlegrounds, to give us the tactical edge while taking advantage away from those seeking to do us harm.

## ISSUES

> Architecture is inescapably a political art, and it reports faithfully for ages to come what the political values of a particular age were. Surely ours must be openness and fearlessness in the face of those who hide in the darkness. Precaution. Yes. Sequester. No.
>
> SENATOR DANIEL PATRICK MOYNIHAN

The immediate physical response to the attacks of 9/11 was to use just about anything heavy or strong enough to stop vehicles dead in their tracks or keep them from violating standoff zones. The most common temporary element used was probably precast jersey barriers (used for traffic control on roadways), followed closely by large precast planters known as *bunker pots* (actual potted plants seemed optional). This spectrum broadened to include precast drainage structures and dry-well rings (materials intended to be buried in the ground) installed along the perimeter and major paths in highly visible areas around our government institutions in Washington, D.C. See Figures 1-1, 1-2, and 1-3, for example.

Street closings utilizing temporary jersey barriers were employed to restrict vehicular traffic accessibility to potential high-profile targets. Often, large security vehicles with drivers were used to function as sliding gates to allow the passing of emergency or other authorized vehicles through openings between the barricades. The lack of a coordinated approach to these closings resulted in an increase in traffic congestion, a compromising of emergency services access, and disruption of pedestrian movement. One of the most notable streets affected

**Figure 1-1**
Jersey barriers and police barricades installed to provide temporary perimeter security. Courtesy of the National Capital Planning Commission.

**Figure 1-2**
Temporary barriers require additional security personnel to help make them effective. Security personnel have to be taken from their routine patrols and responsibilities. Courtesy of the National Capital Planning Commission.

**Figure 1-3**
Access to the Capitol is controlled by vehicular barriers, along with portions of a highway barrier in front of the guard booth, "bunker pots," and precast concrete drainage structures on the sidewalks. Courtesy of the National Capital Planning Commission.

**Figure 1-4**
Layers of redundant security barriers in front of the White House. Courtesy of American Society of Landscape Architects.

was Pennsylvania Avenue, which was closed in front of the White House. There now is general agreement that Pennsylvania Avenue should remain closed and the area transformed into a pedestrian promenade fitting of its symbolic and historical significance. In most respects, this will be an improvement over the proliferation of temporary barriers that have sprung up in this area.

Many observers reacted negatively to the aesthetic and psychological impact of widespread deployment of precast concrete *anything* sprinkled throughout our most valued landscapes. This got the attention of not just designers but government officials, who realized security measures taken to protect our people and institutions must not inflict damage to our physical, historical, and cultural heritage. Security cannot be achieved by sacrificing the very values and qualities that we seek to protect. Figure 1-4 illustrates the extensive barrier system erected around the White House.

Deploying the quickest and cheapest means of protection when heightened security first arises is understandable, but the

**Figure 1-5**
The Washington Monument became the "poster child" of temporary barriers that became long-term fixtures, remaining in place for over a decade. Courtesy of American Society of Landscape Architects.

likelihood of these temporary measures becoming permanent should concern us all. Knee-jerk responses can actually increase the perception of threat and instill fear, rather than promote a secure feeling. A measure of terrorist success is if we all become terrified. In addition, erected barriers greatly affect the way people interact with their institutions, government, and each other. Figure 1-5 highlights the barriers surrounding the Washington Monument that, while offering protection, also diminish the view of the obelisk rising from the ground to the sky.

The tendency to default to an extreme fortress-like design response must be avoided. A parallel can be drawn to the American criticism of the Soviet public architecture during the Cold War years. During this time, our nation was critical of the lack of openness of Soviet government buildings and embassies, and the perception that secretive discussions and decisions that were hidden from other nations, as well as the Soviet people, were architecturally manifested in these fortress-like structures. We need to be sensitive that if we move too far toward this architecture of high walls, imposing building facades, restriction of public access, and intimidating security checkpoints, we will be gravitating towards an architectural symbolism that we found so inherently objectionable just a few years ago.

The immediate responses to heightened security come at a high price: the price of temporary physical improvements, increased personnel and overtime costs, and the psychological impact on our citizens. It is imperative that we integrate security measures in our designs for new construction (or the retro-fitting of existing facilities) in a way both effective and flexible to varying levels of threat. This can be achieved using familiar site elements while providing effective security in a seamless, trans-parent manner.

It is possible to have good urban design principles employed—creating beautifully rich streetscapes and public urban plazas—in an approach that also addresses the need for enhanced security. These objectives need not be mutually exclu-sive. The direct and indirect costs of employing temporary barri-ers and security measures and maintaining them over time can be reinvested in a coordinated and comprehensive approach uti-lizing good, permanent security design. Over the long term, this will prove to be a cost-effective approach in dollars as well as to protect and express the democratic ideals that serve as the very foundation of this country's existence. The premise that our gov-ernment is "for the people, and by the people" cannot be under-estimated or sacrificed in the name of security. Instead, it must challenge us to come up with creative design responses that meet the needs for enhanced security as well as reinforce our nation's fundamental civic values.

## DAWN OF A NEW SITE DESIGN ERA

A number of reports were issued during the 1990s and early twenty-first century in response to attacks on United States interests at home and abroad. Many of the reports generated were initiated at the federal level, but the criteria and guidelines developed are certainly applicable at the state/local and public/private levels. The reports acknowledge that terrorist attacks can take many forms, but the overwhelming threat—accounting for more than half of incidences—is from bomb-laden vehicles. This type of attack (for which stand-off zones were created) is thought of as the easiest way to cause extensive damage, loss of life, and possible progressive collapse of the structure being attacked. The emphasis on creating secure setbacks is one of the primary responses required in order to enhance security of a potential target.

The most referenced and useful reports issued through 2004 are as follows:

- *Urban Design Guidelines for Physical Perimeter Entrance Security: An Overlay to the Master Plan for the Federal Triangle,* issued by the General Services Administration (GSA), published by Sorg and Associates in Washington, D.C. May not be available to the general public; for more information, contact Sorg and Associates at (202) 393-6445.
- *Designing for Security in the Nation's Capital,* issued by the National Capital Planning Commission's (NCPC) Interagency Security Task Force, November 1, 2001.
- *The National Capital Urban Design and Security Plan,* October 2002, issued by the National Capital Planning Commission's (NCPC) Interagency Security Task Force, October 2002.
- *Security Planning and Design: A Guide to Architects and Building Design Professionals,* copyright 2004 by the American Institute of Architects. Published by John Wiley & Sons, Inc., Hoboken, NJ.

In addition to the resources noted above, the Federal Emergency Management Agency (FEMA) is creating a series of reference manuals called the Risk Management Series. The publications are directed at man-made disasters. The objective of the series is to reduce physical damage to structural and nonstructural components of buildings and their related infrastructure, and to reduce resultant casualties during conventional bomb attacks, as well as during attacks using chemical, biological, and radiological agents. Publication 430, *Primer for Incorporating Building Security Components in Architectural Design,* due out in 2005, will provide guidelines for providing security against physical attack through perimeter, site, and building design. It will be a companion volume to FEMA 426, *Reference Manual to Mitigate Potential Terrorist Attacks Against Buildings,* which provides basic guidance for site and building security design. FEMA 430, however, will focus on site and building design in more detail and with particular reference to achieving acceptable security with minimum impact on community, site, and building amenity, attractiveness, and day-to-day functionality. For more details, visit the following website: www.fema.gov/fima/rmsp.shtm.

For landscape architecture practitioners, the *NCPC's National Capital Urban Design and Security Plan* is a comprehensive reference of security design proposals for downtown Washington, D.C., prepared by several of the most prominent landscape architecture and architecture firms practicing in the United States, including Chan Krieger and Associates, Devrouax & Purnell, EDAW, Michael Van Valkenburgh Associates, Olin Partnership, Peter Walker & Partners, and Wolff Clements and Associates, Ltd. Excerpts from this publication appear in Chapter 4.

What makes these documents so significant is their recognition of varying levels of security for buildings based on their likelihood of being a terrorist target. Not every building or facility needs the same level of protection. The varying levels of threat classified in this document, and the strategies for response presented, are the basis for the consideration of a broader spectrum of design elements to be used to establish perimeter security. Figures 1-6, 1-7, and 1-8 show recommendations for security zones.

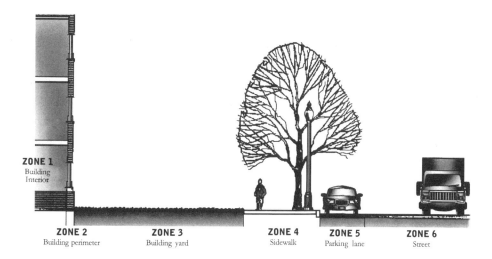

**Figure 1-6**
GSA Security Zones. Courtesy of the National Capital Planning Commission.

# General Security Design Solutions

## Building Security Zones

The "Urban Design Guidelines for Physical Perimeter Entrance Security: An Overlay to the Master Plan for the Federal Triangle," prepared by GSA, presented the concept of security zones. Each of these zones, ranging from the building's interior to the public streets around the building, have different security risks and responses. These can be translated into different architectural, landscape, and streetscape responses to meet these security needs.

GSA's security zones include:

- Zone 1: Building Interior
- Zone 2: Building Perimeter
- Zone 3: Building Yard
- Zone 4: Sidewalk
- Zone 5: Curb or Parking Lane
- Zone 6: Street

Zones 1 and 2 are related exclusively to the architecture of the building, and are not the subject of these guidelines for physical perimeter security. Zone 6 is not subject to these guidelines, except insofar as a decision in the case of Pennsylvania Avenue near the White House must be made – whether to open the street or to keep it closed.

Zones 3, 4, and 5 are related to both the public right-of-way and the surrounding design context of the building. Design guidelines are recommended for these zones.

## Zone Prototypes

Extending GSA's concept of security zones, the Task Force developed prototypes for the exterior zones of buildings.

## Building Yard (Zone 3)

The building yard is that portion of the site located between the building wall or façade and the sidewalk or public right-of-way. The following are recommended guidelines for security measures to be implemented in the building yard security zone:

- Design security measures, such as gatehouses and other entry facilities, to relate primarily to the design of the building.
- Design other security measures to relate to the character of the surrounding area.
- Do not impede pedestrian access to building entries or pedestrian circulation on adjacent sidewalks.
- Use raised planter or building terrace as vehicular barrier, and integrate landscaping and seating.
- Use bollards, light standards, planters, or other furnishings to secure gaps and limit vehicular access through pedestrian access points.
- Plant trees in the yard adjacent to the sidewalk to create a double row of trees flanking the sidewalk.
- Incorporate furnishings and amenities into the building yard.

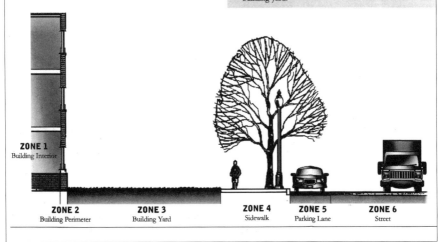

**Figure 1-7**
Recommendations for Building Yard (Zone 3) security design enhancements. Courtesy of the National Capital Planning Commission.

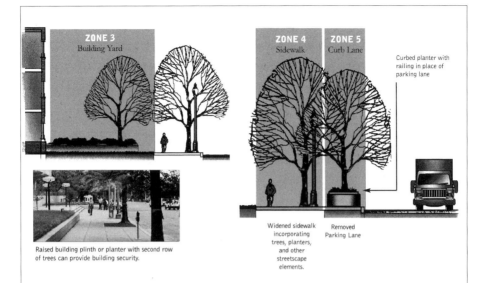

Raised building plinth or planter with second row of trees can provide building security.

Widened sidewalk incorporating trees, planters, and other streetscape elements.

Removed Parking Lane

## Sidewalk (Zone 4)

The sidewalk zone is located between the building yard and the curb or parking lane. The following are recommended guidelines for security measures to be implemented in this zone:

- Design security measures to relate primarily to the character of the adjacent special street or contextual zone.

- Incorporate security design within the design of street lighting, planters, bollards, streetscape amenities (seating, trash receptacles, flagpoles, kiosks, signage, drinking fountains, water features, etc.) and landscaping.

- Do not impede pedestrian access to entries or pedestrian circulation on the sidewalk.

- Integrate planters and bollards into the overall streetscape design.

## Curb Lane (Zone 5)

The curb or parking lane is that portion of the street adjacent to the curb. The following are recommended guidelines for security measures to be implemented in the curb or parking lane security zone:

- Eliminate parking in this lane where warranted by the security risk assessment.

- Eliminate curbside loading zones and service access.

- Incorporate the curbside lane into a widened sidewalk zone.

- Reserve sections of the curb lane for exclusive agency use where such use can be controlled and monitored.

A sidewalk that incorporates security measures should not look like a sidewalk to which security has been added. Instead, security measures should be incorporated into the overall design of the streetscape.

**Figure 1-8**
Recommendations for Sidewalk (Zone 4) and Curb Lane (Zone 5) security design enhancements. Courtesy of the National Capital Planning Commission.

## General Services Administration Zone Classifications

Because of the high threat levels attached to many of its properties, the General Services Administration (GSA) has taken the federal government's lead on setting standards for domestic site and building security guidelines. (For U.S. government–owned properties abroad, the lead agencies are the U.S. Department of State's Bureau of Overseas Building Operations in coordination with the Bureau of Diplomatic Security). GSA's approach provides state and local governments and the private sector with guidelines for approaching a comprehensive site security design strategy.

The *Urban Design Guidelines for Physical Perimeter Entrance Security: An Overlay to the Master Plan for the Federal Triangle* report classifies threats with letter designations (A through E), and divides a building and its site into six numbered zones. A-level buildings are considered least likely to be threatened, while E-level facilities require a very high level of protection. The security zones are Zone 1, Building Interior; Zone 2, the Building Perimeter; Zone 3, the Building Yard; Zone 4, the Sidewalk; Zone 5, the Curb Lane; and Zone 6, the Street (refer back to Figure 1-6).

In order to establish an appropriate security level, the various agencies of the federal government were asked to evaluate their facilities in accordance with a number of criteria that would help determine the level of potential threat. The criteria considered a building's symbolic importance, critical nature of operations, consequence of an attack, and a look at the surrounding site conditions.

Site factors that influence a building's level of potential threat need to be considered, as well. In looking at stopping a vehicle, the angle of approach and ability for the vehicle to accelerate to a high rate of speed need to be evaluated. A building's existing setback from the site perimeter is a consideration. The Interagency Security Task Force established a desired setback of 50 feet and a minimum setback of 20 feet. Many existing buildings may not have this desired minimum setback, and security alternatives need to take the existing setbacks into account. Existing buildings must be evaluated for their structural ability to resist the effects of a bomb blast. As each building is unique architecturally and structurally, a determination must be made related to the ability to harden the building's structure, if that option is even possible, and balance that against the cost of those modifications.

When this threat classification system was applied to the many public and federal buildings in Washington, D.C., most buildings fell into either a C or D threat level. To put this threat level into perspective, a perimeter barrier for a D-level building must be able to stop a 6-ton vehicle traveling 50 mph impacting perpendicular to the barrier.

The GSA's establishment of security zones includes a wide range of alternatives that can be used in each of the zones to address the established level of threat. The suggested site elements allow for combinations and placement resulting in creative designs that can complement the surrounding architectural character of the area.

In looking at the security zones exterior to the building, Zone 3, the Building Yard, is defined as the area between the building's facade and the sidewalk. Security elements for this area should complement the building's architecture. Where the building yard provides the necessary setback from the street, perimeter barrier elements can be placed along this zone's outer edges or adjacent to the sidewalk. No additional perimeter security would need to be provided beyond that point (see Figure 1-7).

Zone 4, the Sidewalk, is defined as the area between the edge of the building yard and the curb or parking lane. This zone should be kept as free as possible so as not to impede pedestrian movement. It is in this area that many of the street amenities that we all feel familiar and comfortable with can be located in a hardened form to provide perimeter security. In cases where there is a need to extend the setback distance even further, the sidewalk can be widened, possibly eliminating the parking lane. Where parking remains, barriers must allow for the opening of car doors and safe access for the passengers from their car to the sidewalk. A minimum distance of 18 inches is recommended between the edge of the curb and adjacent sidewalk site elements.

Zone 5, the Curb Lane, is the lane of the street used for curbside parking, passenger drop-off, and service vehicles loading and unloading. In special situations, this lane can be removed for the meaningful widening of the sidewalk thus increasing the setback distance to the building. However, parking and other needs of nearby buildings, along with street traffic flow, must be taken into account before removing this curb lane (see Figure 1-8).

In new construction, a site can be enhanced with security features integrated in the architecture. Structural modifications and building hardening can be applied to existing facilities, and the measures employed can be unique for every structural and architectural design. This approach, if at all possible, is usually very costly. As such, most efforts to enhance the security of existing facilities and structures focus on the exterior zones (3 to 6), making them extremely important. Although a wide range of recommended approaches to site security are presented, particularly for Zones 3 and 4, a few general principles are imbedded in these recommendations. One, that security measures taken should relate in character and context to the adjacent buildings and surrounding area, and should not impede pedestrian access. Another is the recommendation that enhanced security should be provided through the integration of design elements, rather than be dependent on one single element.

## THE GOAL OF GOOD SECURITY DESIGN

Good security design should integrate site and building security elements and associated technologies into a design that makes high-quality and enjoyable spaces, especially in the public realm.

A good security design integrates the building's purpose and operation with protection against real and likely threats through design, technology, and operational activities and procedures.

A comprehensive and coordinated security design is most easily developed and implemented when a new building is being constructed on a site. New construction allows for a security-thoughtful site selection and location for the building on that site. One of the most obvious benefits is that the proposed building can incorporate structural features to meet desired security objectives in the initial design phase. Another closely related benefit of a new building is the ability to have the floor plan design reflect the location of personnel and various critical functions in a way that minimizes the potential impact of a terrorist event. The location and number of entrances can be designed for good security visibility and to minimize the need for monitoring by security personnel. The location and design of vehicular entry points, a critical point of vulnerability, can be carefully considered to screen vehicles and their occupants without disrupting pedestrian travel on the sidewalk. Electronic detection and surveillance equipment can be incorporated into the new design to maximize their effectiveness. And finally, the coordination of site security design concepts and elements can be incorporated, at the earliest stages of design development, to complement the building's physical security design features. Security concerns have made the integration of building architecture and site design increasingly critical. The key to taking full advantage of the security design opportunities that new building construction offers is the collaboration of all the related professionals at the beginning of the design process and each step along the way.

The development of a comprehensive physical security design response in an existing building, even as an afterthought in new construction, is generally a more difficult task. The structural modifications and building hardening that can be applied to existing buildings can be unique for every structural and architectural design. The retrofitting with structural modifications to resist terrorist attacks can interfere with the existing building's basic functions, place constraints on the usable space within the building, compromise the original design intent, and have a negative impact on the building's architectural character and aesthetics. This approach, even when possible, is usually very costly and must be balanced with the results of the threat analysis for the building. As such, most efforts to enhance the security of existing facilities and structures focus on the area between the building facade and the street.

Whether coordinated with new construction or modified to enhance the security of existing buildings and facilities, site elements used to restrict vehicular access and define pedestrian circulation are extensive and varied. Some of these amenities include bollards, major trees (with and/or without tree guards), benches, planters, bike racks, information kiosks, bus shelters, overhead structures, signage, and flagpoles. These are among the more common elements used to provide vehicular barriers along the street and effective perimeter security.

Building plazas and public gathering places can use these site amenities as well, along with raised planters, changes in elevation (i.e., steps, ramps, and railings), walls, fences, colonnades, statues, and fountains. All of these site amenities can enhance and complement the character of an area and architecture of adjacent buildings. These features provide a meaningful reason for widening pedestrian sidewalks while providing an important increase in the setback distance between the building and vehicles along the street.

Moreover, people are comfortable with these familiar design elements as components in our landscape, and they are thus important tools to be used strategically to enhance site security. These security enhancements will safely allow people to gather in our public and civic spaces, taking part in a wide variety of positive activities. Each of these elements can be beautifully designed and carefully sited, with their commonplace, everyday character disguising their protective role. However, the most successful implementations consist of a combination of many elements rather than any one element. One should think of the vocabulary of site amenities as separate threads woven to create a durable fabric, resulting in a rich streetscape as well as enhanced security.

# A Framework
# for Understanding
# Site Security

For the past decade, design and planning professionals have become increasingly concerned about the deleterious affect of ad hoc security interventions hastily installed at public locations after significant terrorist attacks, such as the destruction of the Murrah Building in Oklahoma City in 1995 and the World Trade Center Towers on September 11, 2001. Precast concrete barriers of all imaginable configurations were placed around the most significant and symbolic public places in America, projecting an image of fear and insecurity. Fortunately, these were only temporary measures intended to respond to an immediate threat and easily removed when either the threat was reduced or more thoughtful permanent measures were installed.

*In recent years, the proliferation of makeshift security measures has had an alarming effect on the historic beauty of the Nation's Capital. Even before the 1995 bombing in Oklahoma City, Washington's streets and public spaces had become an unsightly jumble of fences and barriers. Since the September 11 terrorist attacks, the situation has only become worse with more street closing and more concrete barriers. The National Capital reflects the spirit of America, but today in Washington we look like a nation in fear. We now have a condition that must be addressed to protect our values as an open and democratic society. We urgently need a comprehensive urban design plan that provides adequate security while at the same time enhances the unique character of the Nation's Capital.*

*Source:* "Message from Richard L. Friedman, Chairman, Interagency Task Force," in *Designing for Security in the Nation's Capital,* October 2001, National Capital Planning Commission's Interagency Task Force, Washington, D.C., publication: http://www.ncpc.gov/publications/publications.html

There is no single industry standard or set of governmental regulations guiding the selection and installation of site security features. Although design, engineering, and building firms are developing expertise in this area, there is no one-size-fits-all rule that will provide a high level of security for every project site. And each site does not need the same level of security. So, how can we achieve an appropriate level of security for a given site and fully consider the wide range of design options while security standards are still evolving?

The answer is: *Adhere to the basics.*

## THE BASICS: PROFESSIONAL RESPONSIBILITIES

Although clients may be looking to our profession for answers and safety guarantees, there is no formula of security features and programs that will ensure 100 percent safety against natural disasters or violent attack. Sometimes, the best-case scenario will be to minimize the potential damage caused by a natural disaster or violent attack.

- It is incumbent on both security professionals and designers to accurately inform our clients about the costs, benefits, and limits of security design interventions as part of a comprehensive security program.
- All permanent security design interventions requiring significant installation, operation, and maintenance costs should be tailored to an articulated threat and be part of a risk management program developed in concert with an experienced security professional.

## UNDERSTANDING THE RANGE OF THREATS

When a designer incorporates security into a site plan, it is important to consider the wide range of potential threats to the site and its users, as well as the likelihood of each threat occurring at the site. Permanent and/or expensive site security interventions should be aimed at threats deemed likely to occur, not frightening but unlikely scenarios.

The discussion of threats in the news media today covers a wide range of potential concerns. For any given site, the range of threats could include any of the following:

- *Health, safety, and welfare threats.* This includes natural disasters, faulty building and construction practices, unsafe working conditions, and poor maintenance of public areas.
- *Nonviolent crime.* Theft of real or intellectual property, industrial espionage, or cyber-crime. This type of crime requires internal and external access controls, vetting people given access to the site, and an internal crisis management team to evaluate reality, cost, and source of any theft.
- *Internal or workplace violence.* Some violent crime arises from sources inside the organization. These threats often call for appropriate human resources policies, positive labor/management relations, emergency management plans, and layered access controls within the site.
- *Chemical, biological, and radiological attacks.* The intentional or unintentional release of hazardous chemical, biological, or radiological agents into public areas is a serious threat. The largest threat comes from research, government, pub-

lic infrastructure, or industrial facilities where these materials are stored, manufactured, processed, or manipulated, or from individuals with access to these facilities. Good security requires careful vetting of individuals with access, sophisticated venting and other mechanical and waste disposal systems, access controls, and emergency management plans.

- *Violent crime from external sources.* Violent attacks on the exterior or interior of the site can come from one or more individuals with the intent to harm persons and/or the facility, or to gain publicity through the event for a larger cause.

Landscape architects and others involved in the planning, design, and construction of exterior spaces have long been concerned with *health, safety, and welfare* issues. Indeed, professional licensure requirements are aimed at ensuring that licensed landscape architects and other designers are qualified to create safe, well-constructed, well-organized spaces for their clients.

Nonviolent crimes, such as theft, can be deterred through good lighting, surveillance, visual access to the site, and by programming the site for lively uses that deter criminals. The basic principles of *Crime Prevention Through Environmental Design* (CPTED) seek to deter crime through a strategic use of these basic site design elements and an understanding of occupant behaviors.

However, designers and builders of outdoor spaces have limited influence over deterring or minimizing the damage from most of the other threat categories. These threats usually originate inside a building structure and require specialized security and architectural practices and technologies that are different from what would be used outside a building in a site security design.

But the designers and builders of outdoor spaces can have a significant influence over threats in the final category—violent crime from external sources. Many of these threats originate outside the building where the site design can deter and/or minimize damage while still creating quality public spaces.

## CRIME PREVENTION THROUGH ENVIRONMENTAL DESIGN (CPTED)

Since the 1960s, CPTED's core concept has developed from the work of many leaders in diverse disciplines, including sociologist and urbanist Jane Jacobs, architect Oscar Newman, and criminologist C. Ray Jeffery. Today, many law enforcement and public planning agencies utilize CPTED's methodology to create safe environments with the occupants' participation. CPTED is often applied in commercial, residential, industrial, and educational settings. The National Crime Prevention Institute offers CPTED training.

The central premise of CPTED is that the physical environment plays an important part in promoting crime. CPTED is the design or redesign of an environment to reduce crime through natural, mechanical, and procedural means. CPTED is a multidisciplinary approach to reducing crime and the fear of crime.

CPTED training encourages learning as much as possible about the site, its context, and the needs of the desired occupants. CPTED's basic approach accepts that many disciplines are involved in creating spaces, and the CPTED-certified professional must learn the concerns, strengths, and language of each discipline.

CPTED combines the design of physical space with the physical, social, and psychological needs of desirable occupants of that space to create an environment that encourages desired behaviors and occupants and discourages criminal behaviors and occupants.

Although the goal of addressing enhanced security against terrorist activities may be a different goal, many of the CPTED strategies can be tailored to this purpose. Building on the premise that if site design can make a potential target more attractive, then with changes it can be transformed into a powerful security-enhancing tool.

One basic premise is that if certain conditions create opportunities for terrorist acts, then the reverse can be true—certain site conditions can help prevent terrorist acts from occurring. The key to this targeted approach seeks to redesign the environment to eliminate the possibility or potential damage of a terrorist act. By eliminating these primary terrorist objectives, the terrorist attack is not likely to take place.

CPTED relies on four overlapping strategies to attain this goal:

1. *Natural access control.* Decrease crime opportunity through access control strategies, including organized (e.g., guards), mechanical (e.g., locks), and natural (e.g., appropriate spatial definition). These approaches seek to deny criminals access to the crime target and to create a perception of risk of detection by the authorities.

2. *Natural surveillance.* Facilitate observation of the site by desired occupants to deter crime and increase the perception of risk of detection by the authorities. This can be done in a number of ways, such as creating good visual access to all areas of the site, including from the street and from inside buildings.

3. *Territorial reinforcement.* Create and/or expand the desired users' sphere of influence so they develop a sense of proprietorship that deters undesired users of the site. This can be through the use of common site elements—street furnishing, lighting, paving, signage, and so on—that signal the beginning of a defined space that is regularly occupied by a community of individuals. This principle has been refined through many applications in public housing settings where there has been a strong emphasis on reclaiming territory for law-abiding occupants.

4. *Target hardening.* Target hardening, where needed, through site design strategies, and formal access control and surveillance measures.

Some common CPTED strategies include the following:

- Provide clear border definition of controlled space.
- Provide clearly marked transitional zones of space (public—semi-public—semi-private—private).
- Relocate gathering areas to places with good natural surveillance and access control.
- Place desired activities in currently undesirable locations to serve as magnets for desired users.

- Place activities that currently occur in "unsafe" areas in safer locations to break the cycle of undesired behaviors associated with the activities.
- Reorganize where activities occur to provide natural barriers between incompatible uses.
- Redesign space to increase natural surveillance through well-placed windows, clear sight lines, and other access controls.
- Overcome a sense of spatial isolation through easy, visible means of communication (emergency intercom/phone stations, personnel on patrol, etc.)

*Source:* Adapted in part from Timothy D. Crowe, *Crime Prevention Through Environmental Design,* National Crime Prevention Institute. Boston: Butterworth-Heinemann, 1991, pp. 30, 106–107.

## UNDERSTANDING VIOLENT CRIME FROM EXTERNAL SOURCES

Violent crime can be perpetrated by an individual or by organized groups.

### Individual Violent Crime

There are many reasons that individuals might resort to violence: they might bear a grudge against someone in particular or an entire organization, they might have radical political or social beliefs inciting them to anger and resentment, or perhaps mental illness has caused disordered thinking leading to violent actions.

If individuals act out a spontaneous feeling of rage, they are likely to use small weapons that are easily accessible on the spur of the moment, such as blunt objects, knives, handguns, and possibly small semiautomatic and automatic guns.

Individuals can also enact premeditated plans to cause harm through stealth, such as letter bombs or cyber-sabotage. These types of attacks are hard to deter through site security design measures, although visual surveillance on the perimeter, access controls at entrances, mail/package-screening procedures, and appropriate IT security measures can announce, delay, or neutralize the attacks.

## Violent Crime by Organized Groups

Organized groups with radical political or religious goals present a very different problem. Most terrorist attacks are well-planned events with multiple goals:

- Cause harm to a selected target and the people in or near it.
- Create publicity for their cause, usually through massive media coverage.
- Disrupt and even destabilize the existing governmental, public infrastructure, or social structures.*
- Earn merit in the eyes of their chosen authority figures.

It should be emphasized that terrorists put a premium on maximizing the publicity associated with the violent attack. Dramatic media coverage, especially gripping images on television, spreads the "terror" that gives these groups a heightened public profile and disproportionate political significance. Therefore, terrorist groups will often seek out targets that can create shocking images that will be readily accessible to the press. Such groups may also focus on targets with political or cultural significance to heighten the emotional power of the attack. Even if the attack is not entirely successful, the terrorist group may count it as a success if there is significant damage and/or publicity to send the message that the target is vulnerable.

## Defining Terrorism

Different governments have had various definitions for *terrorism* over the years. For the purposes of this book, *terrorism* is defined as violent attacks on built facilities by well-coordinated groups who have engaged in extensive research and planning. Site security design can deter and/or minimize the damage created by terrorist attacks. Site security design cannot eliminate the possibility of a planned attack.

---

*Some terrorist groups hope to destabilize society by causing a breakdown of public order, followed by an exaggerated government "crackdown" to impose order, which violates individual civil rights sufficiently to foment a rebellion against the government by a now-oppressed citizenry.

## Organization of Terrorist Groups

Terrorist groups generally organize in small groups called *cells.* Cell leaders communicate with each other, authority figures of the overarching organization (if there is one), and with other anarchist groups with shared goals or enemies. Lower-level cell members may receive training, but they might not have knowledge of specific plans for attack as they are being developed. Their job is to be loyal foot soldiers, and they may be responsible only for their role in a planned attack. This dispersed organizational structure makes terrorist cells flexible organizations that are hard to infiltrate.

## Funding and Weapons of Choice

As with any organization, terrorist groups must pay for members' lodging, food, and tools of trade, such as weapons, bomb-making materials (both bought and stolen), training materials and instruction, computers, phones, and travel expenses. Terrorist cell members may contribute their own income, funds may be provided by allied criminal organizations and fraudulent "charitable" organizations, and some terrorist groups gain income through kidnappings for ransom. Many terrorist groups

### SETBACK VERSUS STANDOFF

Security professionals and military personnel use the term *standoff.* A *standoff distance* implies a controlled buffer zone that allows a target under attack to hold aggressors at bay. However, when landscape architects create public spaces that contribute positively to the urban form, it is useful to employ the term *setback. Setbacks* are a longstanding urban design strategy that performs like standoff zones. Terminology is a powerful tool for creating the correct tone and goal for the project. Using *setbacks* instead of *standoff* zones reminds the designer, the client, and the site's users that the design must create good "people places" that measure up to the dignity of the site's context, program, and/or symbolic meaning.

## THE EFFECTS OF BOMB BLASTS

The high-speed projectiles and overpressure that result from bomb blasts cause injury and death. Of particular concern are the glass shards formed when glass explodes. Even safety glass, which normally breaks into noninjurious pellets, does not behave so well during a blast. Instead, it breaks into thousands of pellets, each with sharp edges flying at near-supersonic speed.

Overpressure is a less commonly known but equally deadly result of bomb blasts. When a bomb detonates, an immediate chemical change takes place. A nearly instantaneous conversion of chemical matter to heat and energy causes a heat wave, an atmospheric overpressure blast wave created by a supersonic expansion of gases, and a seismic event (transmission of a blast wave into the ground and outward). Compared to the blast wave, the heat is transmitted a fairly short distance, but it can ignite combustibles close to the blast, resulting in fires. The front of the blast wave, however, forms a wall of highly compressed air that can travel as fast as 1,150 feet per second, or 784 miles per hour.

When a blast wave meets a structure, it wraps around all surfaces of the structure for less than a second. The forces are very great, and the larger the building, the greater the effect. Whereas a smokestack might survive a blast because the blast wave wraps around it so quickly, an adjacent building might be destroyed because the blast wave exerts pressure on the buildings for a far longer time.

Another factor affecting damage is *distance;* the closer the blast is to a structure, the greater the damage. The initial period of extreme overpressure is followed by a reverse blast wave of almost equal intensity as air rushes back into the vacuum created when the initial blast blew the air away from its point of origin. This process of air compression and resumption of equilibrium creates two blast waves, both highly destructive.

Following is a list of vehicles and their general delivery capabilities in pounds of TNT and the amount of atmospheric overpressure at 30 feet and 100 feet from the blast's point of origin.*

| Vehicle Type | Lbs. Charge | At 30 feet | At 100 feet |
|---|---|---|---|
| Compact car trunk | 250 | 182 psi | 9.5 psi |
| Large car trunk | 500 | 367 psi | 15 psi |
| Panel vans | 1,500 | 1,063 psi | 33 psi |
| Box trucks | 5,000 | 2,900 psi | 100 psi |
| Single-tractor/trailers | 30,000 | 9,290 psi | 593 psi |
| Double-tractor/trailers | 60,000 | 13,760 psi | 1,150 psi |

Adult humans can withstand only about 30 psi to 40 psi of overpressure before their lungs collapse. Death is certain at 100 psi to 120 psi. However, death can occur at pressures as low as 10 psi with infants and the elderly.

A person on the opposite side of a building from a blast is not protected from the blast wave. There is no shadow for a blast wave as there is for heat, as the blast wave wraps entirely around the building. The blast can be mitigated to the extent that the building surfaces collapse (e.g., glass breakage), and the forces of the blast are dissipated by the interior building surfaces.

Total disintegration of a human can occur at pressures above 2,000 psi. Above 5,000 psi, sometimes not even a trace of a person remains. Obviously, it is best to be as far away from a blast as possible. This is why setback distance is important when blast a consideration.

*Charge capacity overpressure information supplied by Hinman Consulting Engineers, Inc., San Francisco, California, a leading blast effects consulting firm.

Source: "Effects of Bomb Blasts" from Security Planning & Design: A Guide for Architects and Building Professionals, copyright 2004 by the American Institute of Architects. Published by John Wiley & Sons, Inc., Hoboken, NJ, p. 29.

rely heavily on donations from sympathetic patrons for their funding.

However, many terrorist groups do not have the funds or ability to carry out sophisticated attack scenarios such as the multiple airline hijackings on 9/11. Most terrorist attacks utilize simple weapons that can be delivered to the target in an easy manner and that will cause major damage in one big impact. This is why approximately 80 percent of terrorist attacks rely on explosive devices hidden in vehicles near target buildings. Bombs can also be concealed in containers or street furnishings at the target site or strapped to the body of a suicide bomber who detonates the device at the predetermined location.

This is why site security design often focuses on keeping a minimum distance between the target facility and potential bomb locations, such as a car or static element on-site. This distance is known as a *setback* or *standoff* distance.

## PATTERNS OF PLANNED TERRORIST ATTACKS

### Target Selection

Attackers may observe several sites before deciding which target to attack. Terrorists want to create an attack scenario that is likely to succeed. If a group determines, through surveillance and research, that a target is well defended — that is, too *hard* a target — the attackers might select another, softer target. One goal of site security design is making your site appear harder than other potential targets.

### Detailed Plans

After choosing a target, terrorists prepare detailed plans based on extensive information gathering about the site and its occupants. They record site characteristics, facility operations routines, who uses the site regularly, and potential access control vulnerabilities. Surveillance and planning may continue for weeks or months, and could include attempts to enter the property to test the level of security on-site.

Good site security design attempts to limit the would-be attackers' choices during the planning stage. For example, if vehicular access were limited to 50 feet from a building façade through a strategic use of site design and furnishings, then terrorists would have to use a car bomb large enough to be effective at that distance, or use another tactic. Or, creating consistent visual access to all parts of a public sidewalk denies attackers the ability to conceal an explosive in a hidden area such as an overgrown planter box or a trash can with a fixed lid.

The remainder of this book will focus on specific site design elements to make a building or area more secure.

# Site Security Design Concepts

A thorough site security program includes consideration of basic concepts that assess the security need and guard against a variety of threat scenarios. These basic concepts are as follows:

- Site survey
- Threat analysis
- Site security countermeasures
- Risk management
- Designing to the threat level
- Designing to performance standards

This chapter looks at these concepts in more detail.

## SITE SURVEY

The security professional conducts a systematic inventory of the site in question:

- Structures
  - Type/purpose
  - Uses
  - Construction methods
  - Construction quality
  - Locations of rooms, common spaces, utilities
  - Points of ingress and egress
  - Flow of people and significant materials through the buildings
- Site characteristics
  - Spatial characteristics
  - Significant views
  - Furnishings
  - Gathering areas
  - Proximity to major transportation routes and other buildings
  - Flow of people and materials through the site/access controls

## THREAT ANALYSIS

Threat analysis is a well-reasoned estimate of the threat of terrorist attack on a facility or a group associated with the facility. As discussed in Chapter 2, terrorist groups select their targets carefully to maximize the likelihood of success and to further their goals within the limits of finite resources. Facilities and groups associated with them in a given geographic area will have varying threat levels.

Threat analysis evaluates a given facility's and user's history, current activities, public image, and previously received threats in the context of the current threat environment and known terrorist groups and causes. Thorough threat analyses are conducted by qualified law-enforcement/counterterrorism professionals or analysts experienced with evaluating similar properties.

A professional threat analysis is conducted by a qualified security professional, usually a current or former law enforcement officer, member of the armed forces, or security manager at a private firm. However, neither a *security manager* title nor a background in law enforcement or the military is a guarantee that a particular individual is qualified to analyze threats.

Ideally, the individual should be able to demonstrate experience with both conducting threat analyses and implementing site security recommendations at a facility similar to yours. This person should be able to clearly explain the process he or she will undertake when evaluating your site. There should be methodology that is systematic and consistently applied to all aspects of the site. He or she should also be able to discuss solutions that can be used to secure a site like yours, as well as the cost of implementing, monitoring, and maintaining site security equipment and personnel. After the threat assessment, site survey, and risk management assessment are complete, the property owner/manager and security professional agree on the security management programs that best address the threat within the given budget.

Threat analysis requires a careful study of assets, threats to those assets, and the probability that the threats could become real. When conducting a threat analysis, a security professional reviews several questions in detail. These are covered next.

### WHAT ASSETS IS THE CLIENT TRYING TO PROTECT?

- Personnel
- Property
- Significant assets associated with that property (work product, reputation, symbolic value attached to the client's name or location, etc.).

### WHAT KINDS OF ACTIONS COULD DAMAGE THE ASSETS?

- Natural disasters or faulty building and construction practices (health, safety, and welfare threats)
- Nonviolent crime—property theft, intellectual property theft/industrial espionage (internal and external access controls)
- Violent crime from sources inside the workplace environment—workplace violence (access controls, human resource services, labor/management relations)

- Chemical and biological attacks (access control, emergency management plans, appropriate mechanical systems, especially for Level 3 and 4 laboratories)
- Violent crime from sources external to the workplace

WHAT IS THE LIKELIHOOD THAT THE ACTIONS MIGHT ACTUALLY OCCUR, BASED ON THESE FACTORS?
- Threats received by the client
- Threats to the client's kind of business or activities
- Threats to the client's or the site's symbolic value to the client, the larger community, or known ideologically motivated terrorist groups
- Publicly known associations that could generate a threat
- Precedents of attacks carried out against similar entities or locations
- Public relations value of attacking a particular asset
- The neighbors' threat levels

WHAT ARE THE VARYING THREAT LEVELS ON ADJACENT PROPERTIES?
- Security measures should be tailored to the particular site characteristics and threat level.
- Adjacent properties could carry very different threat levels.
- Assess the threat to the client's site and any additional threat concerns generated by adjacent properties.
- If neighbor properties have a site security program in place, work with them to learn what ramifications it would have for the client's site.

## INTEGRATING A SECURITY PROFESSIONAL INTO A DESIGN PROJECT

*"Integrating a Security Professional into a Design Project" is excerpted from Chapter Nine of* Security Planning and Design *by the American Institute of Architects, edited by Joseph A. Demkin. This material, written by Joseph Brancato, ALA, was created specifically for architects. It is included here because it offers valuable and well-articulated advice that is applicable to all stakeholders in the design process.*

Regardless of firm size or focus, effective integration of security into architecture practice touches upon various business issues in a firm's operation. Such issues include acquiring needed skills and resources, identifying and selecting security professionals, contracting for security services, and determining professional liability and other insurance coverage.

### Acquiring Skills and Resources

At this point, there are few formalized initiatives to help architects enhance their security education or training. However, much information about security is available, although there is no single clearinghouse for data. Design professionals generally work on their own to acquire skills, resources, and information through research and networking and by attending conferences, seminars, and workshops.

### Security Consultants

Security consultants provide management consulting services specializing in security; loss prevention or security training; and security equipment system design, evaluation, and specification. Some security consultants provide architecture and design services to clients and architects. However, the focus of security consultants' efforts is to determine the security-related needs of their clients and to provide advice, information, and recommendations to clients. Security consultants offer their services to market or industry, by type of services, or by type of asset to be protected.

*Certified Protection Professionals.* Architects are turning more often to a relatively small but qualified cadre of security professionals known as Certified Protection Professionals (CPPs), who are certified by ASIS International. These individuals generally have broad experience in the public and/or private sectors and, more often than not, bring a wealth of design project experiences to the architect. An increasing number of CPPs specialize in complex security design and integration projects, offering their services through practices similar in scope and depth to the architect's own practice.

*Physical Security Professionals.* ASIS International is developing and introducing a certification program for an additional group of security professionals whose primary responsibility is to conduct threat assessments; design integrated security systems that include people and procedures; or install, operate, and maintain those systems.

*Blast Design Consultants.* Few architecture firms have experience designing structures to resist the effects of bomb blasts. Blast design consultants offer analysis and design services to mitigate the direct and secondary effects of blast loads on structure. The blast consultant usually works with the architects and the structural engineer during the design phase of a project, but the collaboration also extends to other engineering consultants and landscape architects. While there are no certifying bodies for blast consultants, such consultants should have specific background and experience pertaining to the structural behavior of buildings under blast conditions.

*Engineering Consultants.* An increasing number of engineering consultants are adding security design and engineering capabilities to their practices. Although engineering consultants are typically members of a project team, their participation may be deeper on security-enhanced projects. Decisions regarding building systems, construction materials, air filtration systems, and other elements can affect the cost and effectiveness of implementing security-enhanced design.

*Professional Security Systems Integrators.* Because a building security management system is another form of building control, many clients and developers prefer to integrate the security function into one seamless building control system. Professional security systems integrators can help achieve such integration, which in turn allows for higher security, lower costs, and greater convenience. Because these individuals are well versed in all aspects of building security technologies and a variety of building systems, they can provide valuable input during security audits and during the design phase and can even install security systems after the design has been completed.

Reputable integrators are authorized manufacturer installers trained in the systems they install, and they may warrant the entire system (as opposed to a manufacturer's warranty for pieces of the system). Most clients hire security designers with objective viewpoints to complete their systems design and then bid the design to at least three qualified integrators who can meet the specifications. Some clients, however, prefer to go directly to a single integrator, mainly because of a prior relationship or experience.

Although many security consultants have federal government, federal law enforcement, or military backgrounds, an increasing number of security experts emanate from the professional engineering, private security, or aerospace security sectors. As with any area of expertise, seeking recommendations from fellow practitioners is a good way to find a security specialist. In addition, several organizations (e.g., ASIS International and the International Association of Professional Security Consultants) can offer guidance and potential candidates. Security industry directories are another source. These include the *Security Industry Buyers Guide* (www.security-management.com) and the *SDM/Security Buyers Guide* (www.securitymagazine.com). Security directors at larger client organizations can also be a source of recommendations.

### Qualifications of Security Consultants

As a rule, a security consultant should have demonstrable experience in performing threat, vulnerability, and risk analyses. Look for a consultant with a commanding knowledge of the security equipment types, systems integration methodologies, and engineering practice required to successfully translate a client's security needs into working security systems.

It is important to confirm the credentials of a security consultant (e.g., CPP, registered architect, or professional engineer). Some consultants may have professional membership in organizations such as ASIS International or the International Association of Professional Security Consultants. However, there may be only a limited number of consultants among the membership of these associations with the qualifications for a specific project type.

Although truly experienced security consultants offer a breadth and depth of expertise that can be applied to virtually any type of project, it is best when a consultant has experience working in a client's project type. Personality is another consideration because the security consultant will work with sensitive information, collaborate with a variety of team members with different perspectives, and have to communicate accurately and comprehensively. A final consideration is whether a consultant carries professional liability insurance, and, if so, in what amount.

Other items to discuss with candidates include the following:

- Consultant's affiliation with security products and services, if any
- Type and extent of consultant's liability coverage
- Amount of time consultant dedicates to security consulting
- Types of work the consultant subcontracts to others
- Outstanding claims or lawsuits against the consultant
- Consultant's prior experience on a project of similar type and scope

*Cost of Consulting Services.* The cost of security consulting services varies, depending on the nature and scope of the project. Typically, however, security design services range from 6 percent to 12 percent of the projected installed cost of the security systems. The fee may include security programming and a report, although a fee for these services may be charged separately. Likewise, bidding and negotiation services and construction administration services are either priced separately, or wrapped into the cost for total security design and integration services. In either case, construction administration costs can vary significantly, depending on the number and type of site visits required.

### Contracting for Security Services

Clients may contract for security evaluation and planning services through the design professional, or obtain those services directly from a security consultant or specialist. Regardless of the contractual arrangement, these services should generally provide some or all of the following:

- A security assessment, consisting of asset, threat, vulnerability, and risk analyses
- An existing facility survey of the project site, building exterior and interior, mechanical and electrical systems, data and communications features, and an assets inventory
- A facility analysis of how the building is to be occupied and how its various functions will support owner and tenant operations
- A risk assessment, which determines the level of security required by the client for the project
- Development of security design requirements

As in any agreement, it is important to properly characterize the scope and nature of the services the architect will provide. As always, an architect should avoid providing any professional services that are beyond his or her expertise. Whether the security consultant is retained by the architect or directly by the client, the architect should determine the extent to which the consultant is insured for professional liability. When the architect retains the security consultant, the architect should also confirm whether such services are covered under its professional liability insurance policy. (Liability insurance is discussed in more detail below.)

One reason for a client to seek security enhancements is to reduce insurance costs, and tenants in a building with enhanced security levels may get reductions on their insurance rates to cover their losses. Many leading insurers have professionals on staff schooled in risk management who are more than willing to assist their clients with risk mitigation. Working with these individuals may help reduce insurance premiums.

When security services are part of the architect's services, the scope can be delineated in the architect's contract with the owner—for example, in AIA Document B141, Standard Form of Agreement between Owner and Architect. AIA Document B205, which is the scope document for Part 2 of the B141, offers a possible scope of security services.

When an architect engages a consultant to perform a security assessment or assist with security design and engineering services, documents from the C series of AIA documents can be used as a basis for defining the architect-consultant relationship. These agreements included C141, Standard Form of Agreement between Architect and Consultant; C142, Abbreviated Standard Form of Agreement between Architect and Consultant; and C727, Standard Form of Agreement between Architects and Consultant for Special Services.

### Professional Liability Insurance

In professional service agreements, it is important for architects to properly characterize the scope and nature of the services they will provide. They should also verify with their insurance carrier whether their liability coverage includes security services. Whether retained by the architects or directly by the client, the security consultant should be required to provide a reasonable level of professional liability insurance.

Historically, legislatures and courts have had little occasion to provide guidance on the legal aspects of designing for enhanced security, and this area of law is much in flux. Following are a few steps architects can take to protect themselves:

• Obtain knowledge of security adequate to meet your firm's professional responsibilities.
• Use care in qualifying consultants for security services.

- Address issues regarding provision of security services or inclusion of security features in architectural design that may concern scope, indemnities, and other factors that could affect the architect's liability to clients and others.
- Recognize that clients with high-risk facilities may not want to divulge the security measures and technologies used in their facilities. This could affect the types of information that can be released and the methods used to convey project data.

Ideally, the client will indemnify the architect from claims that might occur as a result of assessment or program evaluation by a security consultant, provided the architect follows a professional standard of care in implementing the consultant's recommendation during design and construction. However, because a third party is not a party to the owner-architect agreement, it can bring legal action if an event causes damages or loss of life or property. An indemnification from the client can provide necessary protection to the architect.

Prior to passage of the Terrorism Risk Insurance Act on November 26, 2002, some carriers that offer professional liability insurance to U.S. design professionals excluded damages caused by incident of terrorism from their policies. The provisions of the act voided such exclusions with respect to foreign acts of terrorism within the United States (except in the case of air carriers, vessels, or occurrences on the premises of a U.S. mission). The insurer had 90 days from November 26, 2002, to advise their policyholders of the additional premium they would charge to provide coverage in conformance with the act. Upon receipt of the notice from the insurer, the policyholder had 30 days to accept the coverage and pay the required additional premium. If the policyholder declined the coverage, the exclusion would apply. Because of the complexity of the professional liability issues, architects are strongly urged to consult both their attorneys and their professional liability insurance brokers and carriers for guidance.

---

*Source:* Text from "Security Planning & Design: A Guide for Architects and Building Professionals" in *Finding a Qualified Security Professional to Conduct a Threat Analysis,* pp. 183–191.

## TERRORISM INSURANCE

The Building Owners and Managers Association (BOMA) International surveyed its members in September 2002 concerning the availability of terrorism insurance. An overwhelming majority of respondents cited difficulty in obtaining adequate coverage at affordable rates, and 27 percent of respondents were unable to obtain terrorism insurance at any cost. Of the 73 percent who were able to secure coverage, 80 percent incurred some or all of the following: higher premiums; caps on coverage; higher deductibles; cancellation clauses of 60 days or fewer; and exclusions for chemical, biological, or radiological acts. Increases in premiums ranged from an average low of about 20 percent to a high of 200 percent. For 69 percent of the survey respondents, a building's geographic location was among the factors that made it more difficult to buy insurance.

The BOMA survey provided clear evidence that insurance coverage for terrorist events has been unavailable at any price for one-fourth of office building customers and that the product that has been available does not meet the needs of building owners and managers. The outlook improved markedly, however, with the November 26, 2002, enactment of the Terrorism Risk Insurance Act. This act nullifies terrorism exclusions on professional liability policies as well as commercial property policies.

The new law, to remain in effect for three years (allowing the private insurance market for terrorism coverage to develop), makes available up to $100 billion in federal funds to cover losses from a terrorist attack. The federal government is to pay for 90 percent of losses above the deductible (set at 7 percent of premiums the first year, 10 percent the second year, and 15 percent the third year). Among the provisions of the law, insurers are to offer coverage for losses from terrorist acts that is basically the same as the terms, amounts, and limitation applicable to losses from other events.

*Source:* Text from "Security Planning & Design: A Guide for Architects and Building Professionals" in *Finding a Qualified Security Professional to Conduct a Threat Analysis,* p.189.

## SITE SECURITY COUNTERMEASURES

After conducting the site survey, the threat assessment, and a risk analysis, consider site security countermeasures that may deter or repel anticipated threats:

- Personnel to monitor and supervise the perimeter and access control points
- Budget for hiring security personnel, installing security technology, and maintaining physical improvements
- Physical improvements to the perimeter and access control points:
  - Setbacks
  - Physical barriers and perforations
  - Visual surveillance
  - Access control
  - Layered perimeter

### Setbacks

Setbacks, also known as *standoff* zones, are established distances between a target object, such as a building, and the closest point of attack. As already noted, approximately 80 percent of terrorist attacks utilize car bombs, so setbacks are an important tool to reduce the effectiveness of car bombs.

Bombs damage surrounding structures by sending out waves of energy that shatter building materials; structural materials may collapse while smaller pieces of debris flying through the air may seriously injure people in or near the building. Bombs hidden near buildings in vehicles, planters, street furniture, or other containers can cause serious injury and structural damage. Increasing the distance between the origin of energy created by an explosion and built structures reduces the amount of damage sustained by those structures.

Setbacks reduce the impact of explosions near target buildings, hinder the accuracy of projectiles thrown or shot at the target area, and slow the approach of attackers moving toward a building on foot. The property manager/owner may have a predetermined setback for their facilities. Setbacks of 100 feet or more are ideal to make a significant reduction in the effectiveness of perimeter bombs, but such setbacks are often unattainable except in new suburban developments. In urban areas, setbacks of at least 20 feet can be hard to achieve.

Another way to create a setback on a narrow site is to adjust a building's massing so that the upper floors of the building step away from the street or shift the most important functions to areas that will be less exposed should a bomb blast occur on the street level. See Figures 3-1, 3-2, and 3-3.

Some researchers advocate constructing perimeter walls to deflect the energy waves from a bomb explosion. However, there

**Figure 3-1**
The Federal Building in New York City has extensive glazing on the northern façade that creates an inviting and open lobby. Although the lobby comes out to the sidewalk with no apparent setback, the structural elements of the building are actually aligned with the setback of the upper floors, further from the street. This is a good security design strategy within a dense urban setting by using the architecture of the building to establish a setback of structural elements from the street.

**Figure 3-2**
The upper floors of the building are set back from the street to minimize the impact of a bomb blast generated from the street level.

**Figure 3-3**
The southern side of the Federal Building has vehicular access that is protected by a beam barrier controlled by a guard booth integrated into the architecture of the building. The bunker-like look of the guard booth is representative of the level of blast resistance this critical street level facility is built to withstand. The floors immediately above have very small windows and the upper floors again step back to minimize the impact of a street-level bomb blast.

is disagreement about the effectiveness of these walls. Consult your client's security building standards when determining the appropriateness of such walls and construction specifications.

Design strategies for setbacks should be linked with the threat level and tailored to the desired activities in each site area. For example, a setback along a major thoroughfare may require a boulevard feeling with seating areas, plantings, and other street furnishings. A setback adjacent to another property's service area might call for simple fences or removable bollards at key access points.

## Physical Barriers and Perforations

Physical barriers are any combination of built elements that slow or stop people or objects from entering a designated perimeter area. Barriers and appropriate perforations enforce setbacks. Barriers generally include perforations to allow controlled access of vehicles and pedestrians. Security staff may monitor barriers.

Barriers can be composed of movable or permanent elements from 6 inches to 12 feet tall. Some barriers are heavy objects designed to withstand impact from a moving vehicle, while other barriers are easily moved to accommodate changing crowd control needs.

### *Site Design Strategies to Create Setbacks or Physical Barriers*

Setbacks and physical barriers can be created by a variety of design strategies. In new construction, a site can be enhanced with security features integrated in the architecture. This allows the opportunity for the building design to respond to site conditions and be complemented by the design and location of site elements and the setbacks that they create. This coordination is particularly critical in urban environments where it is often impossible to achieve desirable setback distances on all sides of a building. The structures of these buildings can be hardened and smaller window openings can be incorporated on sides of the building where setback from the public street is not feasible. Where the building can be set back further from the street, site elements that provide a secure perimeter allow for use of a more open architecture. This provides an opportunity for more extensive use of glazing materials and architectural fenestration that create an inviting, friendly, and aesthetically pleasing entrance to the building. The best examples of good security design in new construction are the ones represented by the close coordination of the architect, structural engineer, and landscape architect from the earliest phases of design development.

Structural modifications and building hardening can be applied to existing facilities. However, several constraints need to be considered. The first is that the building's design and location on the site are already a given that provide the basis for any security enhancement considerations. Given the broad spectrum of different types of buildings whose construction spans many years and whose technological levels of construction differ widely, it is clear that necessary structural modifications and building hardening measures will also vary widely for every particular structural and architectural design. Thus, modifying an existing building, if at all possible, is usually very costly. In many cases, the impact of these modifications on an existing building's exterior architectural aesthetic or its function is determined to be unacceptable. Therefore, most efforts to enhance the security of existing facilities and structures focus on the area outside of the building, making the site design an extremely important component of the comprehensive security design plan.

A couple of examples of compensatory design responses might include the widening of the sidewalk and the elimination of curbside parking. This can increase the distance between a building's facade and proximity to any vehicles. The widening of the sidewalk offers an opportunity to include a variety of site amenities that can enhance the pedestrian experience while providing perimeter security. Where traffic volume allows, changes in vehicular circulation patterns can be considered that may even result in the closing of a street to vehicular traffic. The closing of streets can provide an opportunity to create wonderful pedestrian malls. Where feasible, these strategies can increase the setback of an existing building from its proximity to vehicles by altering the circulation of traffic, and this can increase a building's ability to resist a bomb-laden vehicle's blast.

The significance of criteria that are currently the basis for federal policy and guidelines is that they allow for varying levels of physical responses to the various levels of potential threat. Buildings requiring the highest levels of protection—because of threat and potential high-speed, unimpeded perpendicular vehicular access—still require the highest (and usually most visible) physical security elements. However, buildings with a lower level of risk can be adequately protected with a much wider array of site elements that have the positive impact of enriching the streetscape while providing the appropriate level of security. These site elements can relate in character and context to the adjacent buildings and surrounding area in a way that seamlessly integrates the security enhancement into the fabric of the area. The best site security design responses include a variety of familiar design elements, rather than relying on the repetition of any one specific element. The integration of these site elements can provide continuity to a streetscape and enhanced security that is virtually transparent without impeding pedestrian circulation or access.

One of the most vulnerable access points for a major terrorist attack is the vehicular access point. As represented by the first attack on the World Trade Center, a bomb-laden vehicle exploding in a garage under a target building can cause devastating damage. In new construction, it is best not to design a building requiring high-level security with parking directly below the building. In existing buildings that already have this configuration, it is advisable to discontinue use of the parking facility. Where this is not possible, use of the parking facility directly below a building that may be a high-profile terrorist target should be restricted to staff and business-related visitors that already have a high level of security clearance. A physical security check of all vehicles will still be necessary (a personnel-intensive task); however, the potential risk is much lower than it would be for an underground facility that allowed parking of vehicles by the general public. These same considerations should be given to above-ground parking areas that would allow vehicles closer to the building, or more sensitive parts of a building, than the setbacks established for the general public's vehicles.

In cases where the highest level of security is required (particularly where buildings require vehicular entry points), heavy-duty fence and locking gates, rising vehicular barriers, beam barriers, and guard booths are still required. However, even these extreme measures to address security can be done in a manner consistent with good design principles.

The rising vehicular barrier is the most common of the elements designed to stop unauthorized vehicular entry. It can be installed as a flush mount onto existing pavements or as part of a shallow foundation system. This heavy-duty steel barrier rises in a matter of seconds to create a triangular-shaped form, hinged at ground level on the protected side, and rising approximately 1 meter (3.3 feet) on the attack side. It can be designed to stop a five- or six-ton vehicle traveling 50 miles per hour dead in its tracks and still remain operational. See Figures 3-4 and 3-5.

**Figure 3-4**
The rising vehicular barrier stopping a truck during an impact test. Courtesy Delta Scientific, Inc.

**Figure 3-5**
The results of a truck impacting a rising vehicular barrier. Courtesy Delta Scientific, Inc.

**Figure 3-6**
Beam barrier with steel cable integrated into the arm, locks down between the concrete anchors to effectively stop a vehicle. Courtesy Delta Scientific, Inc.

Less common (or perhaps less obvious) are cantilever or track grates that can be designed to withstand similar crash criteria. These gates open by sliding back parallel to the opening they are protecting. The gates open and close at a rate of approximately 30 feet per minute, therefore the length of time it takes to complete a full open or close cycle is a product of the gate's width. A gate width can range from a typical opening of 9 or 10 feet, to widths of 30 feet or more. Although they take longer to open, one advantage is that they allow wide openings to be protected from unauthorized vehicular entry, as well as restrict pedestrian travel. One of the obvious disadvantages is the length of time to close this type of gate and the inability to respond to an immediate attack that would require an immediate closing of the access point. However, there are situations where both vehicular and pedestrian access needs to be controlled. This type of gate is well suited for those situations and its value should not be overlooked.

Also effective in meeting established criteria for stopping vehicles is the beam-type barrier. In many ways, it resembles the typical parking lot arm barrier with which we are all familiar, but its ability to stop a vehicle is not visually obvious. The hydraulically powered arm locks down between two crash-rated anchors. What provides its deceptively high strength is the steel cable beam integrated into the arm. The combination of these components creates a highly effective vehicular barrier, as shown in Figure 3-6.

These sorts of barriers at vehicular entry points typically require a gatehouse to monitor their operation and control vehicular authorization and access. The vehicle entry point needs to be laid out in a way that allows several vehicles to line up while awaiting entry authorization without interfering with

**Figure 3-7**
Rising vehicular barrier in a light color, blends with bollards and existing masonry wall to deny access to unauthorized vehicles.

**Figure 3-8**
The large planter directly in front of this rising vehicular barrier prevents a vehicle from accelerating and striking it head on. Instead, a vehicle would have to slow to negotiate the turn, increasing the effectiveness of the barrier. In addition, the planter helps to soften the visual impact of the security design elements between these congressional office buildings.

pedestrians or vehicular street traffic. This ideally positions the gatehouse on the protected side of the vehicular barrier. Gatehouses come in a number of different functional designs and sizes that one would associate with this function. However, in areas of significant symbolic or architectural importance, every effort should be made to design this structure in the context of the building it is serving and the character of the surrounding area (see Figure 3-7). Where a street or other straight portion of road exists that would allow a vehicle room to accelerate to high speeds, it is advisable to design the vehicular entryway with elements that force a vehicle to slow down and turn before reaching the vehicular entry barrier. The slowing of the vehicle to negotiate the turn makes the vehicular entry barrier that much more effective (see Figure 3-8).

New, innovative techniques are currently in development to create less intrusive vehicle barriers on public streets. One approach, in development by designers working with the Army Corps of Engineers, includes a special area of paving five or more feet adjacent to the sidewalk. Below a surface of unit pavers or cobbles, this area's base is composed of compressible aggregate that cannot withstand the weight of an automobile. Any vehicle attempting to mount the sidewalk from the street would sink in this area before reaching the sidewalk. Thus, this paved perimeter on grade with the roadway would act as an effective vehicle barrier without using any vertical elements protruding from the ground plane.

For situations requiring a less extreme security approach, the site elements used to restrict vehicular access, establish a secure perimeter, and control pedestrian circulation are extensive and varied. The list starts with bollards, which come in many shapes, sizes, styles, and materials. Bollards are typically 24 to 48 inches tall and are installed 4 feet on center. Bollards allow some circulation through the perimeter line (pedestrians, cyclists, etc.) while denying vehicular access. Because bollards are installed with significant space between them, they do not form a solid fence or wall. This tends to give the areas protected by bollards a much more open feel, allowing pedestrian traffic to flow without being impeded. Bollards can enhance the basic design principles of character, scale, rhythm, and harmony to a streetscape while providing the necessary perimeter security. Bollards can be fixed, stationary elements, removable or retractable. In low-threat environments, bollards can be installed with minimal foundations to serve as passive pedestrian control measures that do not guard against significant vehicular impact. Or, in high-threat environments, bollards can be installed with significant foundations and interior shafts that meet government standards for impact resistance (see Figures 3-9 and 3-10).

**Figure 3-9**
The bollards installed at the Capitol restrict vehicles but allow pedestrians to pass, maintaining an open and accessible feel to the entry.

**Figure 3-10**
The bollards at the Capitol complement the existing walls and entry piers aesthetically and functionally by protecting the opening between them. The existing walls have had their height extended, using a detail that is very much in the same design context as the original wall, to further enhance security.

Retractable bollards can be lowered into the ground, by hydraulic or pneumatic power, to allow vehicular access to an area. In colder climates, the below-ground assembly can be heated to prevent freezing up in cold weather. Although they can be used to control access to a vehicular entry point, they are used more commonly where vehicles enter on an irregular basis. Typical uses might be to allow emergency or maintenance vehicles into an area while restricting regular vehicular access on a day-to-day basis.

Removable bollards have a locking device that holds the shaft in place with a base that is anchored into the ground. The bollards can be removed with the proper key to unlock the latch. A consideration with the use of this type of bollard is the anchoring base that locks the bollard in place. When the bollard is removed, it is best if the remaining base is flush with the adjacent pavement so the base does not become a tripping hazard for pedestrians. This requires that the locking mechanism be below grade. Having access to the locking mechanism in cold climates where snow and ice are a factor make this type of installation problematic. In any case, the resulting hole with the bollard removed can be a pedestrian safety issue. Removable bollards that have a base flange that extends several inches above the adjacent pavement addresses the climatic access concerns but creates a pedestrian safety concern. A variation on the removable bollard is the collapsible bollard. The collapsible bollard has a locking device that, when deactivated, allows the bollard to be folded down, allowing vehicles to pass. An advantage to the collapsible bollard is that it prevents the bollard from being removed from the site or lost, as can be the case with a bollard that can be totally separated from its base. The locking mechanism can be placed near the top of the bollard, making deactivation easier and making it less susceptible to weather-related factors. Here again, the bollard folded down still sits about 3 or 4 inches on top of the pavement, creating a potential tripping hazard. Given the pedestrian safety concerns with these types of bollards, they are best used to allow emergency or maintenance vehicles into an area on an irregular basis, with the bollard placed back into position immediately after the authorized vehicular entry or exit.

A typical configuration for restricting vehicular access usually employs three or more bollards, depending on the width of the opening. The bollards should be spaced at a distance less than the width of a vehicle, approximately 4 feet on center. Ideally, the spacing for perimeter security should create a situation where an unauthorized vehicle trying to gain access will impact at least two bollards. Bollards spaced every three to five feet adjacent to the street curb create a formidable vehicular barrier, protecting both building and pedestrians on the sidewalk from illegal vehicular access. Bollards have traditionally been used to restrict vehicle access and have therefore accumulated the necessary test data for confirming performance requirements. For situations where the highest levels of vehic-

**Figure 3-11**
Bollards used in conjunction with the building's existing site features to enhance security.

ular impact are required, bollards can be anchored by substantial concrete footings below grade or can even be installed in a continuous-grade beam that helps distribute impact over a greater area. Either of these installations can be tied to the horizontal concrete sidewalk with steel reinforcing, creating a system that offers cumulative resistance, as opposed to depending

**Figure 3-12**
Bollards enforce vehicular setback at this vehicle drop-off for visitors at this congressional office building. Bollards are very effective in situations where vehicles need to be restricted but pedestrians should be allowed to pass freely.

on the strength of just one of the elements (see Figures 3-11, 3-12, and 3-13).

Unfortunately, the bollard has become such a knee-jerk response to perimeter security that its overuse diminishes its design value. Other site amenities can be creatively used to provide perimeter security (lest we become cities of bollards). Some of these amenities include major trees with tree guards, benches, planters, bike racks, information kiosks, bus shelters, overhead structures, signage, and flagpoles. These are among the more common elements used to provide vehicular barriers along the street and effective perimeter security.

However, these types of amenities do not come with data relating to their ability to withstand impacts nor meet established criteria, as they traditionally were not thought of as security elements or vehicular barriers. Currently, many site ameni-

**Figure 3-13**
As attractive as each bollard may be, long lines of bollards can diminish their design effectiveness. In this example, there is no curbside parking and pedestrians do not need access through this area. To include other elements, or perhaps integrate the trees into the line of bollards with an appropriate tree guard, would have provided a variety and design rhythm to this streetscape.

ty manufacturers are developing their products to be integrated into a security design response. As part of this product development, necessary testing and data will become available that will make it easier to determine a product's ability to meet vehicular impact criteria and establish necessary anchoring requirements.

At this point, many installations are tested on a case-by-case basis, and before they can be used to enhance security, they must be modified, or *hardened*, to resist vehicular impacts. This may involve strengthening the element by increasing the size or strength of its components, or the way those components are connected. It most certainly would involve strengthening the manner in which these elements are usually anchored in place.

Landscape architects have used these familiar design elements before, and they can be used again strategically to enhance security. This security enhancement will safely allow people to gather in our public and civic spaces, taking part in a wide variety of positive activities. These gatherings are an important part of who we are as a nation, and we must not let security concerns prevent us from coming together.

All of these elements can be beautifully designed, carefully sited with their commonplace, everyday character disguising their protective role. However, the most successful implementations consist of many elements combined together rather than depending on any one element. One should think of the vocabulary of site amenities as separate threads woven to create a fabric, resulting in a rich streetscape as well as enhanced security.

The use of these traditionally nonsecurity elements allows a great deal of flexibility and creativity in a design response. One strategy in addressing the need to stop vehicles from speeding toward a facility is not to provide those vehicles a straight path whereby they can accelerate to dangerous speeds. Careful siting of elements and changes in grade can be just as effective in preventing a vehicle from attaining a speed that requires a more extreme measure of security. This approach then provides the opportunity to take advantage of an even broader spectrum of common site elements that can withstand impacts of vehicles at less than high speeds.

Seat walls and raised planters (precast and freestanding or cast in place) can be used to create secure perimeters. To be effective, they need to be at least 28 inches high. (If a seat wall is installed adjacent to a street that is 6 inches lower than the sidewalk, the seat wall can be lowered to 22 inches minimum height so that overall change of grade to the street will be 28 inches.) Seat walls need not just be placed parallel to the street. In conjunction with other perimeter security elements, they can be placed at any angle or even perpendicular to the street to create interesting seating opportunities. Wherever seat walls or raised planters are used immediately adjacent to the street, consideration needs to be given to how pedestrians crossing the street can gain safe access to the sidewalk and, if there is a parking lane, how those people open their doors and exit their vehicles. Regular openings that allow pedestrians to get to the sidewalk cannot be overlooked. Where parking lanes exist, these raised walls should be set back approximately 2 feet to allow people to safely exit. At corners, bollards are still the most effective approach to restrict vehicular access but allow pedestrians to cross the street unimpeded.

A wide range of different fence types can be selected to provide perimeter security based on the purpose of the fence, the program of the open space, the architectural context of the area, and the threat level of the target that it is protecting. The fencing that offers the least security is the movable fence type. Movable fencing is composed of easily manipulated panels of metal pipe fencing or chain link fencing on metal pipe frames. The panels can be linked together or stand independently of the adjacent panels. Their posts have flared bottoms that give each panel some degree of stability. The level of stability is sometimes augmented by the addition of concrete blocks that help hold the fence posts in place. They can be waist-high or up to 8 feet tall. The most familiar use of the low pipe rail type of movable fence is to organize in an orderly fashion people waiting in queue lines for special events. The taller chain link movable fence is most often used to keep trespassers out of potentially unsafe conditions such as construction sites. Any security that these types of fences add to a site is more psychological rather than physical. These fences are best used in low-threat environments for temporary crowd control. If used temporarily in higher threat levels, security personnel must monitor these fences closely because they can be easily breached.

In some ways, the *jersey barrier* is a kind of movable fence, although its primary purpose is for control of vehicular traffic. It became the temporary barrier of choice in the weeks and months that followed 9/11. It has substantial mass and weight that make it a formidable vehicular barrier. In order to be effective, jersey barriers must be installed in a fixed manner that allows their weight and bulk to withstand impacts from moving vehicles. If a jersey barrier is laid on a pad to protect expensive sidewalk paving, the barrier will be rendered useless, as it will slide forward upon impact. Unfortunately, as we have seen, these same characteristics have led to them being kept in place far longer than the definition of *temporary* might give the impression. The machinery necessary to move these long precast sections of reinforced concrete makes adjustments to their position a difficult task. Therefore, once in place, rarely do they get moved or adjusted to meet changing levels of threat or circumstances.

Recognizing the popularity of the jersey barrier as a vehicular barrier that can be installed quickly, manufacturers of these concrete barriers are now making them in a variety of styles that make them look less like the highway barrier from which they originated. While not necessarily a good permanent solution to vehicular perimeter security, they represent a very good alternative to the traditional jersey barrier. As these barriers tend to stay in place for quite some time (hopefully as a more permanent security design can be formulated, funded, and implemented), the gesture toward making them more aesthetically pleasing results in a far more acceptable temporary solution than negative impacts of the traditional highway barriers (see Figures 3-14, 3-15, and 3-16).

Simple chain link fence, with and without razor wire on top, is perhaps the most popular inexpensive fixed fencing for low- and medium-threat environments. It acts as crowd control and a deterrent to most trespassers in low- and medium-threat environments. These fences have the disadvantage of being climbable and can be defeated by cutting through several links or the razor wire. One way to address these shortcomings is by specifying a tighter 1-inch mesh in the thickest gage metal wire available. However, cutting significant holes through this kind of fencing requires time, large wire cutters, and concealment dur-

**Figure 3-14**
Precast concrete barriers are being manufactured in different shapes and styles as alternatives to the jersey highway barrier.

**Figure 3-15**
These new-style barriers designed specifically for enhancing perimeter security are generally more appealing than other forms of temporary barriers.

**Figure 3-16**

As permanent security designs await funding, go through the approvals process, or are in design development phase, there is no reason the temporary barriers that are put in place cannot be more aesthetically pleasing.

ing the act. Regular inspection by patrols or surveillance by CCTV cameras can deter or quickly discover tampering. Chain link fencing is rather plain even when specifying a PVC colored mesh as an alternative to the standard galvanized metal fabric. When used in conjunction with more elegant site elements or around architecturally significant buildings, its inexpensive, institutional character can appear to be very much out of context.

Metal fences offer a variety of shapes and styles that can meet varying levels of vehicular impact criteria as well as be aesthetically pleasing and sensitive to the architectural context in which it is installed. Metal fences can be made from aluminum, steel, or cast iron in a variety of different finishes for just about any application. They can be a piperail type fence that emphasizes a strong horizontal line or a vertical picket fence that can create a dignified and elegant appearance in a nonclimbable barrier. These fences lend a more formal or dignified perimeter edge that can be striking decorative site elements.

These fences can be built to the desired strength, depending on the type of materials used, how the components are connected, and the method of anchoring the fence in the footing, curb, or wall. For metal fences required to meet the higher levels of impact criteria, it is best to use a fence that has posts and panels fabricated from solid steel components rather than hollow tubes or pipes of other metals. Additional anchoring of the fence at mid-panel can provide added impact resistance, as can diagonal bracing at each of the posts. Connections should be fully welded or bolts made vandal resistant to ensure that the integrity of the fence cannot be easily compromised. Metal picket fences often utilize sharp decorative features on picket ends, and the ends may bend outward to make climbing difficult.

Building plazas and public gathering places can use these site amenities along with raised planters, changes in elevation (i.e., steps, ramps, and railings), walls, fences, colonnades, statues, and fountains. All of these site amenities can enhance and complement the character of an area and architecture of adjacent buildings, as well as provide a meaningful reason for widening pedestrian sidewalks.

### Adjusting a Building's Massing

The massing of a building can be adjusted to create setbacks in the façade to reduce the impact of a bomb blast. Ideally, the most important personnel and functions should be located in the interior areas most protected for a blast area. This can be done by having the facade of the building recede from the perimeter on ascending floors. It can also be done through a creative use of site design and building massing for a layered perimeter that also provides pleasant outdoor rooms.

### Special Considerations

A great deal of a site element's ability to withstand an impact is at the point of connection to the pavement, curb, or footing. The size of curbs or footings may have to be increased to withstand vehicular impact. An element that might usually be anchored in a footing of concrete typically 1 foot square by 3 feet deep might now require a footing 3 or 4 feet square by 5 feet deep. Site features typically anchored in a footing might even require modification for anchoring in a substantial underground-grade beam to create a more monolithic resistance to impact.

Most of these hardening techniques are invisible to the casual observer, which is the value of using commonplace site amenities to enhance security. However, special considerations are necessary because of the substantial below-grade modifications. The areas that would typically benefit from the use of these amenities as security measures, particularly the sidewalk to the curb line, often have underground utilities running along them that were installed at a depth not anticipating the need for this type of construction. Therefore, before embarking on a security design effort of this type, conflicts with underground utilities need to be studied.

Additionally, the increased size of underground footings, curbs, and grade beams can have disastrous effects on existing trees and can severely limit the development or lifespan of newly planted trees. Damage to the root structure of existing trees should be minimized, and new trees should be provided with ample opportunity for their roots to spread. The use of structural soils, providing both a positive growing environment for tree roots and the integrity to support the pavements above, should be considered.

As this type of streetscape improvement to enhance security would most likely require the removal of sidewalk pavement, the opportunity to maximize a tree's ability to survive the urban environment and become a security enhancement itself should not be missed. The locations of underground utility lines and tree roots are so critical that in some cases they may drive the location and even feasibility of using streetscape elements to enhance perimeter security.

## Visual Surveillance

*Visual surveillance* refers to the security staff's ability to see and/or record events taking place in and near the perimeter area. Security personnel must have visual access to the perimeter area to detect events signaling an imminent attack. Furthermore, visible security surveillance is a deterrent to potential attackers, who may decide to choose a "softer" target.

Effective surveillance is conducted by people on foot or in guard posts maintaining a constant view of the perimeter area. Cameras or other technological devices may be used to extend security staff's view and record activities. In addition, members of the public can become a source of information about activities that are significantly out of the ordinary for a given area.

Typical technologies that facilitate constant visual surveillance include video cameras with static views, as well as cameras that can change views according to commands given by security personnel monitoring the pictures. Images are usually recorded on tape or digitally and saved for a prescribed number of days before being erased. Security personnel should monitor the images, especially images from higher-threat locations, in order to act on signs of imminent violent action.

Even with the aid of surveillance cameras, there is no substitute for security personnel on patrol to observe activities within the protected area and to act as a deterrent for undesirable behavior. Security personnel can be deployed at static guard posts, often located at major points of entry for cars or pedestrians. Guards on foot patrol can roam freely throughout the protected area.

More commonly, foot patrols follow a prescribed route; and at key locations guards must turn a series of electronic or manual switches that mark the date and time. This system ensures that security personnel are patrolling the entire protected area regularly. However, a predictable patrol route introduces the possibility that attackers can predict times when target areas are unprotected. As a result, it is advisable to vary the times and routes of security personnel, especially in higher-threat locations.

In addition to security patrols, surveillance can be introduced through passive means, such as locating windows so that building occupants look at various parts of the controlled area outside the building. Even if occupants are not constantly scrutinizing activities outside, their potential for observing activities can act as an effective and cost-effective deterrent to some antisocial behavior or planned attacks.

There is a constant tension between creating a rich landscape design and providing continuous visual accessibility. Some landscape design solutions may call for intense planting, either on grade or in raised planter boxes. Or, the design palette may call for a pool with submerged elements hidden from view by dark-colored materials and heavy shade. To maintain a high degree of security, guards must be able to see easily and quickly into every area of the site, including planted areas and parts of the site that might otherwise be screened from public view.

## Access Control

Access controls are procedures for stopping, identifying, and/or searching people attempting to gain entrance to a facility. Persons not meeting the criteria for authorized access are denied entrance to the facility.

During typical access control procedures, individuals attempting to gain entrance to a facility by vehicle or on foot are guided to predetermined access points where they may be asked to offer proof of identity and the nature of their business at the facility. Employees and visitors may undergo searches of their vehicles and belongings at other access control points. Visitors may be given limited access to inner perimeters within the facility through color-coded badges and/or escorts.

Access controls are generally grouped in two categories: security personnel and mechanical or technological systems.

### Security Personnel

Security personnel at key access points guide visitors to appropriate entrances; guards identify and search individuals seeking access to the building.

### Mechanical/Technological

Mechanical access control systems include a wide range of technology employed to deny access or control environmental conditions that affect individual behavior. For example, locks and swipe-card systems regulate who can enter or exit at designated access points.

### EXAMPLE OF LAYERED PERIMETER: ATF BUILDING, WASHINGTON, D.C.

In Washington, a $104 million headquarters for the Bureau of Alcohol, Tobacco and Firearms, set to break ground this spring [2002] will be among the first to incorporate all post-Oklahoma City federal recommendations. The 1,100-worker center at Florida Avenue and N Street NE will anchor a new office corridor and a Metro stop when completed by 2005. The project features an L-shaped building and a curving three-story "garden wall" that also serves as a defensive ring. City and federal planners agreed to partly close two streets behind the building to meet the 100-foot-buffer requirement, while still permitting traffic. The government plans to allow public access to cafes or other retailers in the outer wall—away from the building itself.

*Source:* Excerpt from "U.S. Aims to Fortify Its Leased Buildings; Rules Would Affect Cities, Private Sector," [Final Edition], by Spencer S. Hsu, *The Washington Post,* Washington, D.C., March 16, 2002, p. A01.

Inventive landscape architecture design interventions can create access control systems that blend seamlessly into the landscape. Through site furnishings, grade changes, plantings, signage, lighting, and framing intended views, people can be guided to intended ingress/egress areas while still enjoying a pleasant outdoor environment near the building.

Good lighting adds to the perception of safety by increasing visual clarity during evening hours. The farther a person feels he can see clearly in an otherwise darkened area, the safer he feels, because potential threats can be detected sooner. Lighting the edges of rooms, corridors, and entries encourages individuals to use the entire space, not just the center. This causes people to "claim" these areas for accepted uses while discouraging antisocial behaviors that typically prefer to be hidden from view.

Metal halide lights give off a whiter light that illuminates vertical planes at farther distances than orange or yellow high-pressure sodium lights commonly used by traffic engineers. This is important because faces are illuminated on the vertical plane. Metal halide lights allow pedestrians to identify faces and other physical details sooner than high-pressure sodium lights. This increases both the safety and perception of safety in a given area, as well as aiding security personnel patrolling a given area after dark.

### Layered Perimeter

A layered perimeter can be thought of as concentric "rings" of increasing security measures around the facility's most important areas. Security procedures implemented in each layer of the perimeter are tailored to each layer's existing activities and threat level. The layered perimeter is implemented by utilizing the previously discussed security measures along with other procedures in varying combinations and levels of intensity.

The public encounters the exterior ring of security in the perimeter abutting public roads or adjacent properties. Individuals may experience increasing levels of access controls and visual surveillance as they enter the building and approach interior spaces.

## THE FIVE COMPONENTS OF RISK MANAGEMENT

Risk management involves five major functions: risk avoidance, risk reduction, risk spreading, risk transfer, and risk retention.

*Risk avoidance* is the process of limiting or eliminating opportunities for loss. This is accomplished by reducing the number of activities or exposure to loss. It is also accomplished by the complete alteration or cessation of human activities and functions that are vulnerable to risk. This is a negative approach that is justified only through cost–benefit analysis that indicates a greater potential loss than gain through the continuance of an activity.

*Risk reduction* occurs through what is referred to commonly as procedural security. Loss possibilities are offset through dramatic alterations of the process of accounting for or controlling human functions. Checks and balances are implemented to increase the likelihood of exposure or to reduce the opportunity for someone to steal or to break the law.

*Risk spreading* is the diversion of resources and assets for the purpose of lowering loss exposure. Distance, location and time are used to create the spreading of assets. Barriers are also included in this concept of risk management. Security engineering and physical security approaches are inherent in the spreading and denial of access.

*Risk transfer* is the fundamental aspect of insurance. A large group of individuals share a common risk, such as a property or casualty loss. Health insurance is a direct form of risk transfer.

*Risk retention* is the conscious acceptance of the potential for loss. Potential losses are not covered necessarily by insurance, nor by other means of security. The owner or individual simply assumes the possibility of a loss.

Risk management is inherent in the operation of any business. It is also inherent in the operation of a community or neighborhood. Without acknowledging it, most people assume the risk of criminal victimization. But they are less likely to continue to assume that risk once they have been victimized.

*Source:* Timothy D. Crowe, *Crime Prevention Through Environmental Design*, National Crime Prevention Institute (Boston: Butterworth-Heinemann, 1991): p. 25.

| Table 3-1 | | | | |
|---|---|---|---|---|
| *Threat Level/Type* | *Terrorism/ Chem-Bio* | *Violent Crime* | *Petty Crime* | *Natural Disaster* |
| High | | | **X**<br>Security<br>Performance<br>Standards/Design<br>Responses 11–15 | |
| Medium | **X**<br>Security<br>Performance<br>Standards/Design<br>Responses 1–5 | | | **X**<br>Security<br>Performance<br>Standards/Design<br>Responses 16–20 |
| Low | | **X**<br>Security<br>Performance<br>Standards/Design<br>Responses 6–10 | | |

## RISK MANAGEMENT

Risk management balances the client's ideal site security needs (derived from the threat analysis, site security survey, and a review of countermeasures) against the amount of risk that the client is willing to absorb, deflect, or transfer based on financial resources, operational needs, and institutional goals and values.

Clients may find that they must absorb a certain level of risk because of the high cost of security measures over time or because implementing the ideal security plan would hinder operations to an unacceptable degree. Altering operations to reduce the threat level or implementing site security design measures are ways of deflecting risk. Or risk can be transferred through insurance strategies.

## Designing to the Threat Level

Temporary security measures that mar the beauty of our most dignified public spaces are understandable after major terrorist attacks. However, when permanent security measures are implemented, the threat level associated with each location should guide the site security design.

When dealing with multiple sites in an area, it is possible to categorize each one as high, medium, or low threat based on standardized criteria, with the understanding that the threat can be rated higher or lower based on the threat level of adjacent properties (see Table 3-1). Government agencies have adopted threat level definitions; check with the client for preexisting definitions that may apply.

The threat level can guide performance standards for site security elements at project sites. For example, sites rated as low threat might have low-key performance standards such as minimal vehicular setbacks, good lighting, and visual accessibility throughout the site. A high-threat location could require larger setbacks, plantings that obscure the location of certain offices, and a path system that closely regulates pedestrian circulation as part of the access control program.

## DESIGNING WITH PERFORMANCE STANDARDS

Rather than mandating a one-size-fits-all program of site security design elements, landscape architects should work with property owner/managers and security professionals to understand the intent of the adopted security plan. Designers should ask, "What do we want the site design elements to do as part of the security program?" (e.g., maintain a given setback for vehicles, maintain visual access to key areas for visual surveillance, encourage pedestrian movement in some areas but not others as part of the layered perimeter or access controls). Designers should creatively incorporate security performance standards with quality design strategies to create beautiful, high-quality spaces worthy of the public realm.

## SUMMARY: TOWARD EFFECTIVE AND FLEXIBLE SECURITY STANDARDS

- Design and build to the threat.
- Include security professionals, engineers, and designers in all aspects of the project to improve communication about shared goals.
- Security professionals should create performance standards for security recommendations that can be achieved through a variety of creative means.
- Rather than a one-size-fits-all rule, future uniform guidelines should provide a range of reasonable security and design responses for a variety of threat environments.

# Case Studies

## HISTORIC CHARACTER

The Southwest Federal Center reflects the ambitions of post–World War II. Although some federal buildings were constructed in the late 1930s, the area retained its local industrial character until the federal government and private developers

---

[1]National Capital Planning Commission, *The National Capital Urban Design and Security Plan,* October 2002, pp. 55–72. Text and images courtesy of the National Capital Planning Commission.

E Street looking toward the Capitol.

transformed the area in the 1960s with new buildings that espoused the architectural and planning tenets of Modernism. Office buildings by architects including Marcel Breuer now dominate the area.

The Southwest Federal Center has not realized the integrity and coherence that was envisioned for it, although components of large-scale public and private sector development, such as L'Enfant Plaza and the 10th Street promenade, were completed. As is typical of that era and style, many of the modern buildings are set back from the street by plazas on structure. Because of the setbacks, raised roadways, plazas on structure, and the ramps for underground parking, the nature of the pedestrian experience is, for the most part, less than optimal.

The Department of Agriculture South Building is one of the most significant examples of federal government expansion during the 1930s (and was once considered the world's largest office building). In addition, the area's earlier industrial character is still evident in rehabilitated warehouses and in the elevated railroad tracks that bisect the precinct. Some of the federal buildings serve industrial purposes, including the Bureau of Printing and Engraving and Paul Cret's 1934 Heating Plant.

Maryland Avenue, one of L'Enfant's original avenues, is not clearly discernable today because of the grade separation for the railroad tracks along the Maryland and Virginia Avenue rights-of-way and the 1970s modernist design approach of siting buildings in large plazas with a poor relationship between building and street. The avenue is not enhanced by distinguished buildings or embellished by streetscape treatments in the manner of other avenues in Washington. The views along the right-of-way are not focused or shaped due to a lack of attention to good urban planning principles that would reinforce the edges.

## EXISTING CONTEXT

Large federal headquarters, often with associated large plazas, characterize the Southwest Federal Center area. Although the initial development of this area reflects the McMillan Plan and the stripped classicism of the Federal Triangle, the majority of

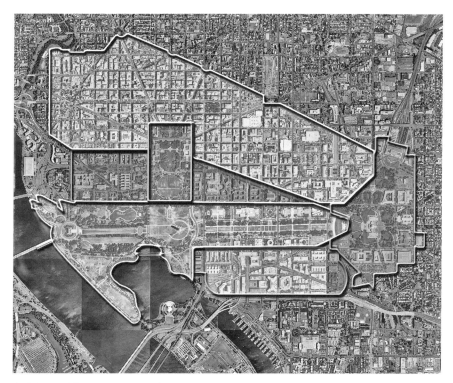

Aerial view of Southwest Federal Center.

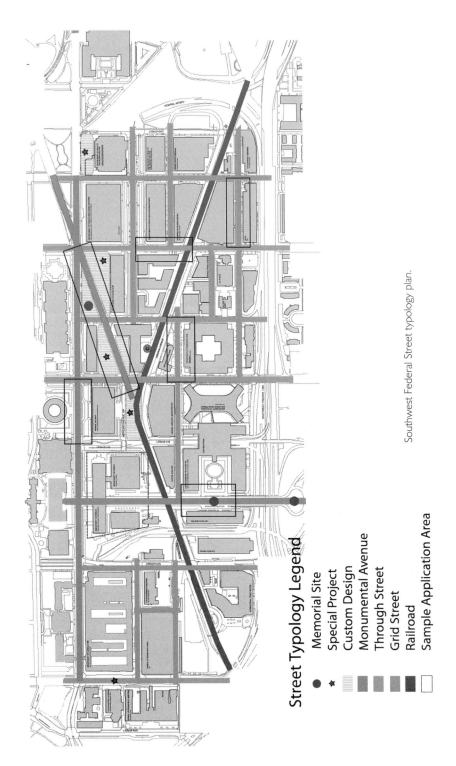

Street Typology Legend

● Memorial Site
★ Special Project
Custom Design
Monumental Avenue
Through Street
Grid Street
Railroad
☐ Sample Application Area

Southwest Federal Street typology plan.

the buildings are characterized as mid to late twentieth-century modern architecture. Maryland Avenue was intended to run diagonally through the center of the area but was truncated after two blocks by the B&O Railroad.

Streetscape designs should be developed and evaluated in relation to the 10th Street promenade design study and to existing urban design projects under study, such as the Southwest Waterfront redevelopment. Designs should repair the isolated and disconnected condition of this area by emphasizing pedestrian and vehicular connections and improving pedestrian circulation patterns. Streetscape design has the potential to unify the appearance of this area more than any other within the Monumental Core.

The provision of perimeter security measures in the Southwest Federal Center area is complicated by several different street and building typologies. Many of the buildings with a high-level security requirement have minimum setbacks and may require curb or parking lane removal to provide a minimum acceptable standoff distance. Given that several of the north-south streets are major connector streets, a detailed traffic analysis and parking assessment is required prior to the removal of curb or parking lanes in this area. These studies must identify appropriate mitigation strategies.

The Southwest Federal Center area is characterized by the following:

- Seventy thousand people work in the area daily.
- Most of the buildings are either owned or leased by the federal government.
- Architecture is not uniform in scale, style, or quality.
- Building setbacks are limited and varied.
- The area suffers from a lack of streetscape design, landscaping, and pedestrian amenities.
- The quality of the environment is perceived negatively.
- There are few through streets, and most are only a few blocks in length.
- Parking is extremely limited.
- Circulation is difficult and uncoordinated.
- Many tourists form their first impression of Washington when arriving by metro in this area.

Given these characteristics, particularly the conflicting combination of minimum setbacks and existing traffic and parking limitations, creative design solutions and strategies to improve safety, mobility, parking, and aesthetics must be developed and implemented.

### Independence Avenue

Independence Avenue frames the southern edge of the Mall and is one of the capital's major ceremonial avenues. Although it shares some of the grand character of Constitution Avenue, Independence Avenue has been neglected and weakened as a ceremonial street. Streetscape design and application of streetscape elements can strengthen the character of this avenue as a ceremonial street and gateway.

### Maryland Avenue

Maryland Avenue is currently in a state of neglect. New streetscape design has the potential to enhance, strengthen, and improve the prominence of this important L'Enfant street.

### The 10th Street Promenade

In L'Enfant's plan, 10th Street was intended to link the Mall with the waterfront and to be a significant axis. L'Enfant Plaza and the 10th Street promenade were the centerpiece of Washington's Southwest redevelopment. The National Capital Planning Commission's recent *Memorials and Museums Master Plan* identifies a commemorative opportunity on this promenade with a major memorial site at the overlook. The District of Columbia is undertaking a transportation and urban design study of 10th Street. Streetscape design can reestablish the pedestrian character of this street while also anticipating a future connection to the Southwest Waterfront.

### 4th, 7th, and 14th Streets, SW

These north–south streets serve as both vehicular and pedestrian corridors. The design and application of streetscape elements, including security components, can improve both driver and pedestrian experiences on these streets and enable important connections to the city beyond.

### The Baltimore and Ohio (B&O) Railroad

The B&O Railroad currently runs on the rights-of-way of both Maryland and Virginia Avenues, bifurcating the area, disrupting the continuity of streets and ultimately impeding mobility within and throughout the Southwest Federal Center. Ceremonial axes that should provide orientation and hierarchy are blocked, and the perception of the area is diminished. In the Legacy Plan, in NCPC's framework plan for Washington's Monumental Core, *Extending the Legacy: Planning America's Capital for the 21st Century,* the Commission recommends relocation of the railroad from this area. Such relocation could reestablish both avenues.

## DESIGN FRAMEWORK

The streetscape designs proposed for the Southwest Federal Center are intended to establish a coherent design identity for this area, while at the same time improving pedestrian and traffic circulation and providing required perimeter security.

Design principles applicable to streetscape designs for the Southwest Federal Center include:

### IDENTITY
- Introducing streetscape elements unique to the area
- Reversing the current negative perception of the area
- Reinforcing the unique character of the predominantly modern buildings
- Establishing streetscapes that enhance wayfinding

### AMENITY
- Mitigating the scale of existing architecture
- Providing seating and other amenities to enhance the pedestrian experience
- Increasing the overall aesthetic quality of the area through the addition of street trees and the design and placement of plantings, street furniture, and lighting

### TRANSPORTATION

- Establishing a sense of hierarchy among existing streets
- Reestablishing north–south connections
- Developing solutions for the provision of additional parking in the area
- Improving circulation for pedestrians
- Developing a Circulator vehicle service

### SECURITY

- Improving circulation and escape routes
- Providing the maximum possible security standoff distances
- Identifying appropriate security components for application in this area

Streetscape design concepts in the Southwest Federal Center include a green streetscape design concept proposed for Maryland and Virginia Avenues, and variations of planter and hardened bench concepts, applied to the grid streets in this area.

Where security is proposed to be located at the curb, existing trees will almost certainly be impacted. Given that many trees are currently missing, or of questionable health, a new street tree planting effort is integral to all of the streetscape design concepts proposed. This will also help soften the area and provide consistency and identity to these streets.

## UNIVERSAL APPLICATION

The following security components are recommended to be applied throughout the Southwest Federal Center area:

- Bollards at entries and corners (to maintain the free movement of pedestrians)
- Removable bollards, as required, for emergency vehicle and service access
- Retractable bollards and/or gate arms at vehicle/service or parking garage entrances (Gate arms are used where volumes preclude the use of retractable bollards.)
- Guardhouses at vehicular entrances (custom-designed to be compatible with the building architecture)
- Curb or parking lane removal (where required standoff cannot be achieved due to limited setback)
- Traffic-calming devices (to reduce the speed of vehicles)

## Maryland Avenue

Maryland Avenue, and those blocks of Virginia Avenue that parallel the B&O Railroad tracks, are proposed to incorporate a green streetscape design. The green design solution consists of a line of bollards between the street trees. New plantings are introduced in the tree planting beds to soften the introduction of these security elements. Bollards are also incorporated on the sidewalk between the planting beds, at building entrances, and at intersection corners. Hardened benches are used at the ends of the planting beds to emphasize the entrance plazas.

## The 10th Street Promenade

The proposed streetscape design for the 10th Street promenade uses seat planters to create an improved pedestrian scale and to formalize and beautify the street. The planter streetscape design concept incorporates large round and linear precast concrete or stone seat planters on the sidewalk on both sides of the street. Existing drop-off or pull-out lanes are removed and replaced with sidewalk so that these planters maintain a consistent line at the edge of the street. Stainless steel bollards are used in front of the major entrances to buildings and on the street corners.

Because 10th Street is built on structure, large trees cannot be introduced into this streetscape, but large shrubs such as crepe myrtle are recommended to provide scale and elegance. The green median strip also provides an opportunity for the location and design of future memorials.

Special conditions exist in association with the Department of Energy that will require custom-designed solutions in this area.

## Grid Streets

Variations of the planter streetscape design concept are applicable to all of the grid streets within the Southwest Federal Center area. Specially designed seat planters and benches are recommended as the primary security components. Streetscape designs may vary in the design and application of these elements. For most streets, these components are proposed to be located in the removed curb or parking lane. If curb lanes are retained, then the alternative streetscape design concept should be applied.

As illustrated on 4th and D Streets, SW, an alternative streetscape is proposed that does not require the removal of a parking lane. Security elements are located at the curb, and, due to the likely damage to existing street trees in this area, new street trees are recommended throughout. A rhythm of new bollards, street lights, seat bollards, benches, and trash cans provide security infill between the trees.

The Bureau of Engraving and Printing and the Holocaust Museum have designed and implemented permanent security measures on 14th and 15th Streets. Future permanent security improvements on these streets should reflect the design of these existing solutions.

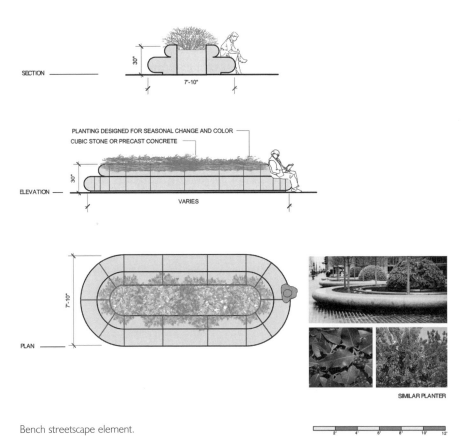

Bench streetscape element.

## SAMPLE APPLICATIONS

Illustrated streetscape security design solutions in the Southwest Federal Center include various applications of the planter and bench design concepts as illustrated: on the 10th Street promenade (adjacent to L'Enfant Plaza); on 4th Street, between D Street and the B&O Railroad overpass; on D Street, between 7th and 9th Streets; and on E Street, between 3rd and 4th Streets. The green design is illustrated on Maryland Avenue.

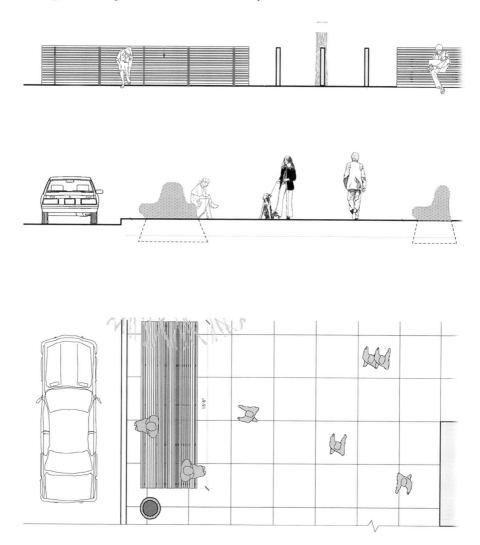

Bench streetscape element.

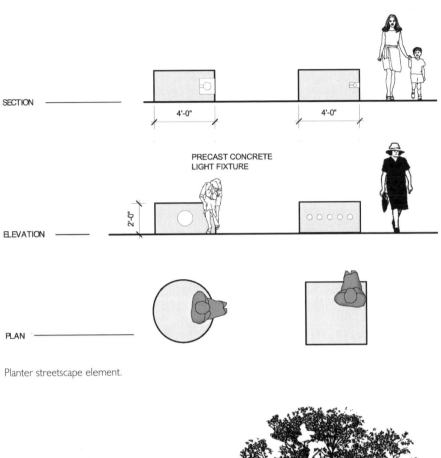

Planter streetscape element.

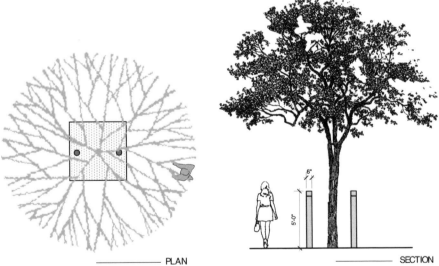

Tree and bollard streetscape element.

## Independence Avenue

Reference Constitution and Independence Avenue Section of the Plan.

## Maryland Avenue Streetscape Design

The application of the green streetscape design illustrated for Maryland Avenue includes tree-planting beds with a double allée of trees and a line of bollards. New plantings are introduced to soften the introduction of these security elements. Bollards are also incoporated on the sidewalk between the planting beds, at building entrances, and at intersection corners. Benches are used at the ends of the planting beds to emphasize entrance plazas.

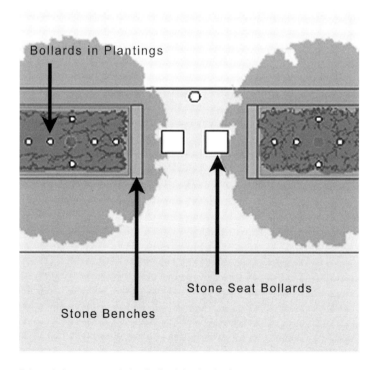

Enlarged plan — green design (bollards in plantings).

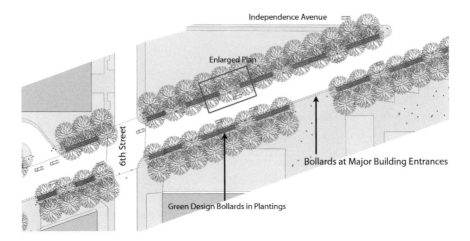

Maryland Avenue sample application—green streetscape design.

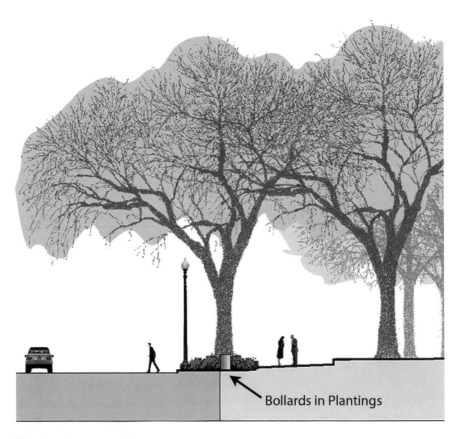

Typical section—green design.

Maryland Avenue: existing conditions.

Proposed Maryland Avenue streetscape design looking toward the Capitol.

## 10th Street Promenade Sample Application—Planter Design

The streetscape design illustrated on 10th Street is one variation of the planter design concept that incorporates a continuous row of seat planters at the curb on both sides of the street. The predominant seat planter is 9 feet, 6 inches wide by approximately 24 feet long, with round seat planters 9 feet, 6 inches in diameter used to create a rhythm, interrupted only by bollards at the major public entrance to the U.S. postal headquarters and on the corners of the entrance and exit drives to L'Enfant Plaza. Existing street lights will remain.

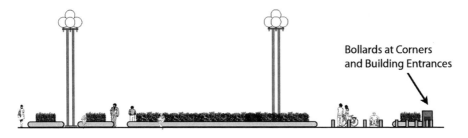

Typical elevation—planter streetscape design

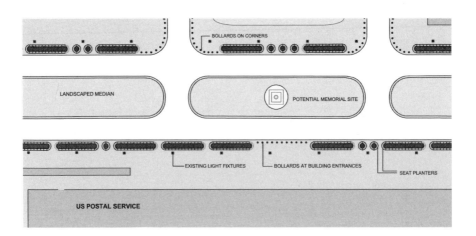

10th Street, SW: sample application—planter streetscape design.

10th Street, SW: existing conditions.

Proposed 10th Street, SW: streetscape design looking south.

In addition, a median is introduced into the existing roadway. This median is illustrated as a landscaped park and may include the location of a future memorial. The median is not required for security, and the design of the median may vary in width and location. Coordination is required with the District's urban design study of this street. A study of the condition and capacity of the existing structure is also required prior to the design and construction of any improvements.

Streetscape elements illustrated for 10th Street include:

- Precast concrete or stone seat planter (2' 6" high, 9' 6" diameter), 42 inches between planters
- Precast concrete or stone seat planter (2' 6" high, 9' 6" wide, 24' 0" long), 42 inches between planters
- Stainless steel cylindrical bollard (2' 6" high, 8" diameter, 4' 0" on center)
- Median, landscape treatment may vary

### E Street, SW

The streetscape design for E Street, between 3rd and 4th Streets, illustrates a security barrier on only one side of the street (adjacent to NASA). Although most streets in the Southwest Federal Center will require security on both sides, there is no need to install perimeter security where it is not required.

The illustrated streetscape security design incorporates a combination of both round and long seat planters and hardened benches at the curb of the expanded sidewalk (over the removed parking lane). Existing street trees are maintained. Lane removal and location of the security perimeter at the relocated curb achieve the best possible security standoff on this street. This streetscape design also helps reduce the scale of the street, slows traffic, and improves the pedestrian environment. Plant materials also help develop character and provide beauty.

#### ADDITIONAL DESIGN CONSIDERATIONS
- Given the limited standoff distance that exists throughout the majority of the Southwest Federal Center, proposed security solutions are either at the existing curb or along a new curb within an extended sidewalk to replace the curb (parking) lanes.

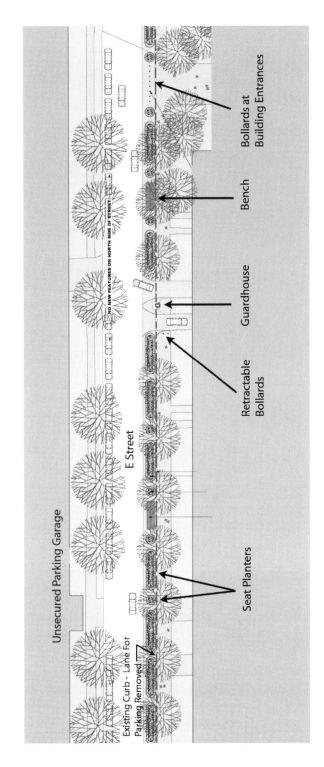

E Street, SW: sample application plan — planter streetscape design.

E Street, SW: existing conditions.

Proposed E Street, SW: streetscape design looking east with parking lane removed.

- Although curb lane removal and expansion of the sidewalk may provide additional standoff, they should be limited to only those streets where absolutely required.

- All curb lane removals must be undertaken in tandem with a comprehensive program to expand short-term parking opportunities through the development of secure, central parking facilities, and to enhance mobility through implementing the Circulator vehicle.

- Streetscape design and implementation for the 10th Street promenade will require analysis of the structural capacity and condition of this elevated roadway.

- The Department of Energy is unique in its security requirements and will require custom-designed security solutions.

- With its narrow sidewalks on Independence Avenue and 14th Street, the Department of Agriculture will require custom designed security solutions.

- Future security improvements on 14th Street should reflect the permanent security installed by the Bureau of Printing and Engraving and the Holocaust Museum.

- Proposed custom-designed security components require engineering and testing to ensure that they satisfy security requirements.

- Underground utility locations are yet to be determined.

## 4th Street, SW

The streetscape design illustrated for 4th Street (between C Street and the B&O Railroad overpass) is a variation of the planter design concept. This streetscape incorporates a row of 9-foot, 6-inch round seat planters located on the extended sidewalk (over the removed curb lane) on both sides of the street. This repetition of planters is intended to provide both identity and consistency to the street. Plant materials are used to develop street character and provide beauty. Stainless steel bollards are located in front of the major entrance to the FEMA building, on the street corners, and at the vehicle service entrances to parking. A guardhouse is also proposed in this location. The existing streetlights are relocated to the new curbs. Existing street trees are retained.

Streetscape elements illustrated for 4th Street include:

- Curb (parking) lane removal
- Extension of sidewalk (over removed curb lane)
- Precast concrete or stone seat planter (2' 6" high, 9' 6" diameter), 42 inches between planters
- Stainless steel cylindrical bollard (2' 6" high, 9' 6" diameter, 4' 0" on center)
- Stainless steel cylindrical retractable bollard (2' 6" high, 8" diameter, 4' 0" on center)
- Gate arm, as per manufacturer's specifications
- Guardhouse, custom designed to relate to the building architecture
- Street trees, infill with the existing species, as required

4th Street, SW: typical section.

**Existing Curb and Parking Lane Removed**

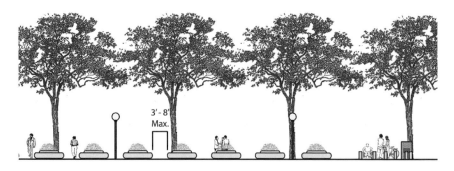

4th Street, SW: typical elevation.

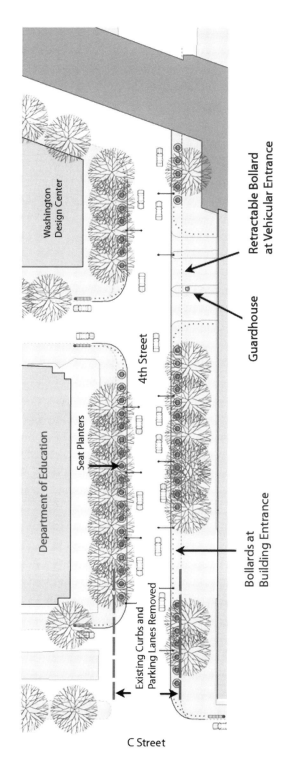

Washington Design Center

Retractable Bollard at Vehicular Entrance

Guardhouse

Department of Education

Seat Planters

4th Street

Bollards at Building Entrance

Existing Curbs and Parking Lanes Removed

C Street

4th Street, SW: sample application plan—planter design streetscape.

4th Street, SW: existing conditions.

4th Street, SW—proposed streetscape design looking south (parking lane removed).

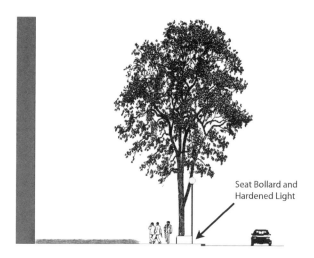

Seat Bollard and
Hardened Light

Typical section D Street alternative approach—bollard and
bench design.

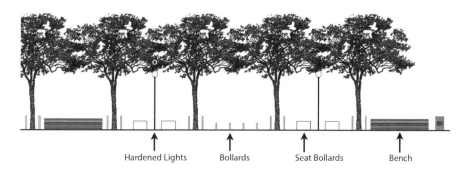

Hardened Lights     Bollards     Seat Bollards     Bench

Typical bollard and bench elevation alternative approach.

## D Street, SW

The block of D Street between 7th and 9th Streets, adjacent to
GSA's regional headquarters and the Department of Housing and
Urban Development (HUD), is illustrated as an example of the
application of the Southwest Federal Center area's streetscape
elements. The curb/parking lane is removed on both sides of the
street. The security barrier on the GSA side incorporates a row of
custom-designed hardened benches with bollards placed

D Street, SW: existing conditions.

Proposed D Street, SW: looking west toward Department of Housing and Urban Development with parking lane removed.

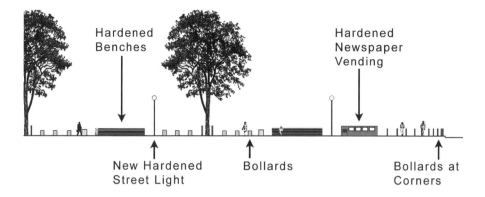

D Street, SW: typical bollard and bench design elevation alternative approach.

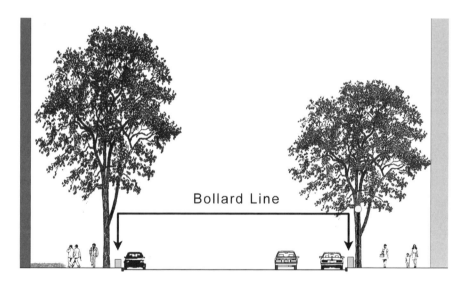

D Street, SW: typical section—alternative approach.

between the benches and in front of the main public entrance to the building. The HUD-side security barrier incorporates a row of 4-foot-diameter precast concrete or stone seat bollards. The typical use of stainless steel bollards on street corners and at vehicle/service entrances is also included. In that few trees currently exist in the narrow sidewalk on this side of the street, new street trees are shown in the widened sidewalk. These trees will help unify the street.

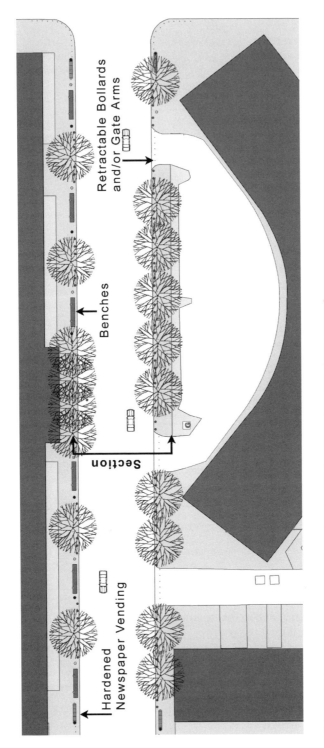

D Street, SW: alternative sample application—bench and bollard design (no parking lanes removed).

This streetscape illustration is representative of the application of these streetscape elements to some of the varying conditions that exist within the Southwest Federal Center (e.g., the narrow sidewalk and block-long building wall of the GSA building, the contrasting building setback, and large ground-level plaza of the HUD building).

Streetscape elements illustrated for D Street include:

- Curb (parking) lane removal
- Extension of sidewalk (over removed curb lane)
- Metal bench (3' 2" high, 15' 6" long), wood or metal slats; one-sided bench 3 feet wide; two-sided bench 6 feet wide
- Precast concrete or stone seat bollard (2' 6" high, 4' 0" diameter), 42 inches between bollards
- Precast concrete or stone seat bollard (2' 6" high, 4' 0" square), 42 inches between bollards
- Stainless steel cylindrical bollard (3' 0" high, 8" diameter, 4' 0" on center)
- Stainless steel cylindrical retractable bollard (3' 0" high, 8" diameter, 4' 0" on center)
- Gate arm, as per manufacturer's specifications
- Guardhouse, custom designed to relate to the building architecture
- Street trees (8" caliper oak), new and infill as required

## Monuments and Memorials: Washington Monument, Lincoln Memorial, and Jefferson Memorial[2]

The National Park Service (NPS) has determined that, in addition to the requirement to provide security (perimeter and entrance) for the Washington Monument, where a security plan is currently under development, perimeter security is required for both the Lincoln and Jefferson Memorials. With the exception of establishing a vehicular barrier at the 17th Street ceremonial entrance to the World War II Memorial, no additional physical perimeter security is deemed necessary at this time for the other monuments and memorials located on the Mall or in West Potomac Park.

## HISTORIC CHARACTER

### Washington Monument

Standing at the cross-axis of the Mall, the Washington Monument is recognized and beloved as a symbol of the city that bears its founder's name. Originally designed by Robert Mills and constructed between 1848 and 1889, the obelisk and grounds were modified and completed by the U.S. Army Corps of Engineers, most notably without the elliptical colonnade that Mills had envisioned for its base. A generation later, the McMillan Plan proposed centering the monument within its setting at the crossing of the two axes of the Mall by embellishing the grounds with an elaborate Beaux Arts–style landscape plan of plantings, terraces, and water pools. The plan was not realized. The monument and its grounds, often referred to as a *greensward,* are at the center of the national capital's monumental core and serve as a natural gathering place for events large and small, public and private. The Washington Monument was one of the first historic properties to be listed in the National Register of Historic Places in 1966. The monument and grounds are recognized as an element of the historic plan of Washington, D.C.

---

[2]National Capital Planning Commission, *The National Capital Urban Design and Security Plan,* October 2002, pp. 37–41. Text and images courtesy of the National Capital Planning Commission.

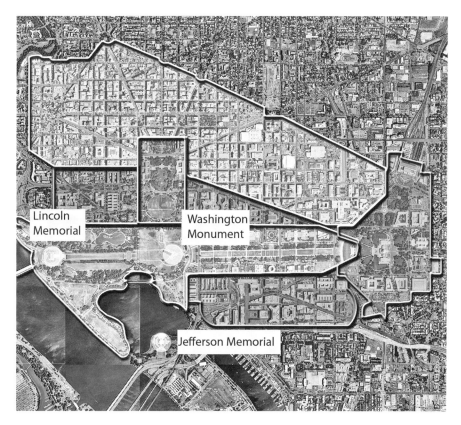

Aerial view of monument area.

Bird's-eye view of the Washington Monument area.

Facing the Washington Monument and the U.S. Capitol, the Lincoln Memorial forms the terminus of the McMillan Commission's extension of the Mall. Henry Bacon's design, ranked among the most beautiful buildings in Washington, is a neoclassical reinterpretation of a Greek temple form with columns in the Doric order. The marble and limestone building, on a high podium with monumental steps, is set within a circle that emphasizes the Mall axis through the elaborate landscaped and terraced base that extends to the Reflecting and Rainbow Pools. Selected through competition, the memorial was designed by 1913 and completed in 1922. Daniel Chester French's majestic sculpture of the seated Lincoln dominates the interior.

### Jefferson Memorial

The Jefferson Memorial forms the southern terminus of the cross-axis of the Mall. The memorial was designed by John Russell Pope and completed in 1942—after his death—by Eggers and Higgins. The marble neoclassical rotunda reminiscent of Jefferson's own designs was famously controversial in its time but is admired today. The formal, classical memorial and its monumental terrace and steps are contrasted by its informal landscape plan by Frederick Law Olmsted, Jr., and its setting on the Tidal Basin. The dome and colossal statue of Jefferson by Rudulph Evans are the focus of magnificent views across the Basin from the White House and other axial points. The steps of the memorial provide magnificent views towards the Washington Monument and the city beyond.

## DESIGN CONTEXT

The Washington Monument and the Lincoln and Jefferson Memorials are surrounded by generous expanses of open space that exceed the minimum required standoff distances determined for these memorials. This response allows for flexibility in the design of the perimeter security solutions for these memorials, including the manipulation of topography and the creation of low walls, planters, and other elements that both complement and defer to their existing landscape and architecture.

## DESIGN FRAMEWORK

Custom perimeter security designs as described in the following sections are recommended for these memorials.

### Washington Monument

The Washington Monument is one of the nation's most prominent and visible symbols and one of Washington's most visited sites. The monument has also been the site of numerous threatening incidents and could be the target of a future terrorist attack. Temporary security at the Washington Monument includes a ring of jersey barriers and a temporary visitor screening facility that is attached to the monument's entrance.

The National Park Service (NPS) has developed a concept plan for perimeter security improvements for the monument. The existing walkways would be reconfigured as a series of partial ovals extending east and west from the monument plaza. These walkways incorporate retaining or plinth walls to serve as the vehicular barrier, and individual removable bollards are located at the intersection of the walkways to allow access by service and emergency vehicles. This design concept is consistent with the

Existing security measures at the Washington Monument

principles set forth by the Interagency Security Task Force and, more specifically, those principles that have been proposed for the design of perimeter security for the monument. The Commission approved the proposed concept design plan on February 7, 2002, and will be considering final approval at a later date.

Proposed plan for the Washington Monument.

Proposed grounds at the Washington Monument.

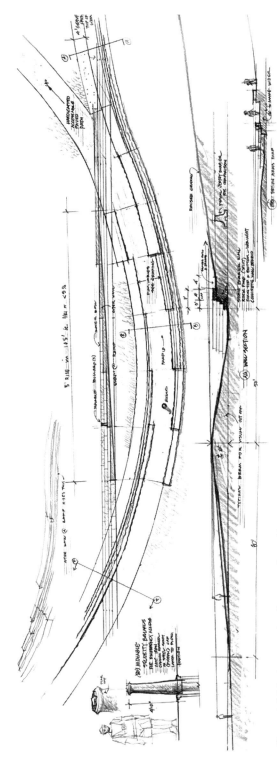

Concept detail of proposed walkways, walls, and berms.

## Lincoln Memorial

The proposed security design for the Lincoln Memorial consists of a low wall that encloses the circular mound upon which the memorial sits. The security perimeter extends across the Mall side of the closed portion of the circular roadway (incorporating bollards and planters) and continues in a line of metal bollards on the Mall side of this road to, and alongside, the steps leading to the Reflecting Pool. The security perimeter is completed across the axis of the Mall by placement of stone bollards at the foot of these steps.

Components proposed for the custom design of security at the Lincoln Memorial include:

- New plinth wall (2' 6" high, 3' 0" wide, length varies), material and finish to match the existing exterior stone of the memorial
- Granite planter (3' 0" high, 1' 0" thick) with five to seven multistem understory specimen trees

Lincoln Memorial — existing conditions.

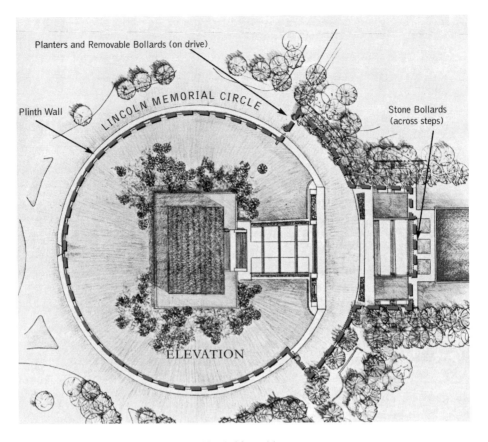

Proposed plan for security elements at the Lincoln Memorial.

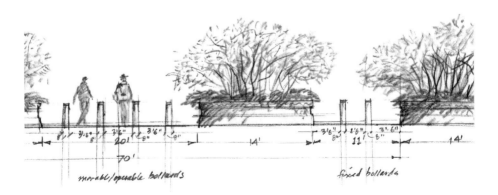

Planter and retractable bollards on Lincoln Memorial Circle.

• Granite bollard (3'0" high, 8" diameter, thermal finish) with
  42 inches clear between bollards
• Stainless steel retractable bollard (simple cylindrical form, 2'6"
  high, 8" diameter) at 4 feet on center
• Regrade slope and sod inside the wall

### Jefferson Memorial

Security design concepts for the Jefferson Memorial incorporate site grading, plinth or low retaining walls, and bollards.
The most effective location for a vehicle perimeter is proposed
along East Basin Drive at the eastern and southern edges of
the memorial grounds. Final design solutions are recommended to incorporate a combination of these elements as dictated
by varying site conditions. Designs are encouraged to fully
integrate the perimeter design as an intrinsic part of the landscape, ensuring that the vehicle barrier is unobtrusive when
viewed in context with the memorial. Security should not
compete with the memorial itself or detract from the pastoral
landscape plan as envisioned by Frederic Law Olmsted, Jr.
Service Drive.

# Symbolically Important Views, Buildings, and Gathering Areas: Pennsylvania Avenue at the White House[3]

## HISTORIC CHARACTER

Pennsylvania Avenue at the White House is one of the most historic and symbolically sensitive places in the nation. The White House, at 1600 Pennsylvania Avenue, lies within President's Park, a special precinct of the nation's capital. Generous public spaces and views, historic buildings and landscapes, and associations to historical events and people characterize this precinct and tell its history. These settings, buildings, and associations have great significance for the American people.

Pennsylvania Avenue is an important element in the White House setting. It traverses the L'Enfant reservation between the White House and Lafayette Park and provides a world-renowned address, public access, open views, and orientation for the White House and other buildings situated on and near it. The route of Pennsylvania Avenue through the reservation was not part of L'Enfant's 1791 plan. It developed as the White House was built, and continued as an informal path in subsequent years. Pennsylvania Avenue was formally made a public street in 1824, the same year that General Lafayette visited Washington and spoke to the public from the park now named in his honor. The segment of Pennsylvania Avenue in front of the White House has been designated a contributing element of the historic street plan of Washington, also known as the L'Enfant Plan.

The layout of Lafayette Park, designed by Andrew Jackson Downing, the noted horticulturist and landscape designer, was implemented in the mid-nineteenth century. Most of the nineteenth-century buildings along Madison and Jackson Places facing Lafayette Park are now executive branch offices, although they were originally private dwellings. Similarly, the buildings on the north side of Pennsylvania Avenue, such as the

---

[3]National Capital Planning Commission, *The National Capital Urban Design and Security Plan,* October 2002, pp. 11–14. Text and images courtesy of the National Capital Planning Commission.

Smithsonian Institution's Renwick Gallery, Blair House, and Riggs Bank, reflect earlier private development near the White House. Lafayette Park is the centerpiece of the Lafayette Square Historic District, designated a National Historic Landmark in 1970. It contains approximately 30 buildings, including the Eisenhower Executive Office Building and the Treasury Building flanking the White House. The 15th Street Financial Historic District and the Pennsylvania Avenue National Historic Site are other designations that document the area's significance.

As in other parts of Washington, and particularly in this area, open space — including the street rights-of-way and parkland — is as significant to the historic setting and as worthy of protection as the buildings. The views and vistas along Pennsylvania Avenue and in all directions to and from the avenue are significant, since they comprise an important aspect of the setting of the White House. Views to and from the radiating avenues were planned by L'Enfant in his design of the White House and they have been reinforced by subsequent architects and designers.

## EXISTING CONTEXT

The Secretary of the Treasury ordered the closure of Pennsylvania Avenue on May 19, 1995, following the recommendation of a blue-ribbon panel charged with reviewing security at the White House to prevent catastrophic damage of the mansion by a vehicle bomb. The security booths and vehicle barriers installed on the avenue and surrounding streets, which were never intended to be a permanent solution, detract from this powerful, historic, and symbolic place. In preparing the recommendations contained in its report, *Designing for Security in the Nation's Capital,* the Interagency Security Task Force analyzed the current and future security needs of the area, past proposals for either reopening or permanently closing the street, and traffic alternatives to the continued closure of the street to normal vehicular traffic.

While pursuing every possible solution that would permit reopening the street, the Task Force, responding to overwhelming and legitimate security concerns, ultimately concluded that the street must remain closed to normal city traffic at this time.

However, the Commission and the Task Force have emphasized that any design for this section of Pennsylvania Avenue must be reversible, and that changes in the security threat or improvements to security technology could result in its future reopening. They further recommended the design and construction of a landscaped civic space that respects and enhances the historic setting and views of the White House.

## CONCEPT DESIGNS FOR CONTEXTUAL AREAS AND SPECIAL STREETS: PENNSYLVANIA AVENUE IN FRONT OF THE WHITE HOUSE

Given its great symbolic importance, the security needs of this portion of the avenue, and its current unacceptable appearance, the Task Force invited four of the country's top landscape architecture firms to submit proposals to create a pedestrian-oriented public space and to accommodate a Circulator vehicle in front of the White House.

The four firms were Balmori Associates and Michael Van Valkenburgh Associates of New York City; EDAW Inc. of Alexandria, Virginia; and Peter Walker and Partners of Berkeley, California.

The Task Force provided the designers with the objectives outlined in its November 2001 report, and with the design guidelines contained in the Comprehensive Design Plan for the White House and President's Park, which were prepared with extensive public consultation by the National Park Service in 1999. In addition to respecting the historic setting of the White House and reflecting the memory of the street's historic use, the Task Force's design criteria required that the proposals do the following:

- Accommodate the staging of inaugural parades.
- Accommodate the Circulator, a new transit system planned for downtown Washington.
- Permit the possible future reopening of Pennsylvania Avenue.
- Permit the possible future construction of a tunnel.

In assessing the submissions, the Task Force examined how well each responded to several urban design objectives including security, circulation, pedestrian environment, visual quality, and historic character.

Based on the recommendation of the Task Force, the Commission selected Michael Van Valkenburgh Associates to proceed with the conceptual design for Pennsylvania Avenue at the White House. The Commission noted that it was selecting a designer and a design approach and that the design concept may be modified and refined as the actual design process goes forward.

## DESIGN FRAMEWORK

The Van Valkenburgh design scheme creates a precinct in front of the White House that uses familiar materials and mediates between the European formality of the L'Enfant plan, the naturalism of Downing's Lafayette Park, and the open setting of the grounds of the White House.

The scheme creates a pedestrian precinct and environment that is welcoming and dignified, and that is able to accommodate multiple uses, including the inaugural parade. It incorporates a simple array of historic Washington light fixtures, stone benches, and other traditional streetscape elements. It preserves the historic axis and existing street pattern and ensures views of the White House.

The concept consists of four primary components:

- Entry plazas at 15th and 17th Streets are formed by the addition of bosques of trees in front of the Treasury Building at the 15th Street entrance and the Eisenhower Executive Office Building at the 17th Street entrance. These plazas provide locations for the required security checkpoints and, together, they frame the area of the avenue in front of the White House.
- Crushed granite granular paving is proposed for the area of Pennsylvania Avenue in front of the White House between Madison and Jackson Places. This pavement is similar to that used on the Mall walkways and in other renowned civic landscapes around the world. This material encourages pedestrian use of the space and acts as a joining element between Lafayette

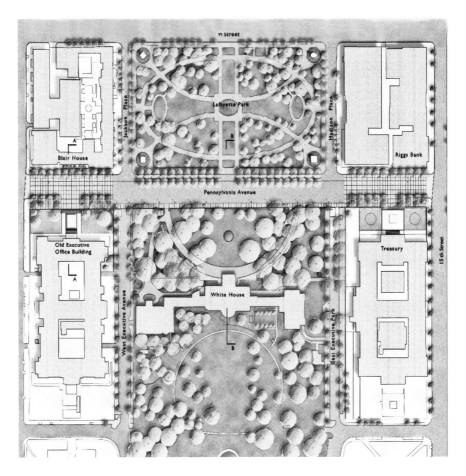

Concept design for Pennsylvania Avenue in front of the White House.

Park and the White House grounds, reinforcing the relationship of the White House within President's Park. The timelessness of the granular paving also references the historic origins of the avenue. The design maintains this central area as an open space, preserving views of the White House and the axial view corridor of the avenue.

• A corridor lined with large trees is proposed on the north side of Pennsylvania Avenue adjacent to Lafayette Park. This corridor serves as a roadway for presidential and visiting dignitaries, motorcades, security and emergency vehicles, and for the proposed Circulator vehicle.

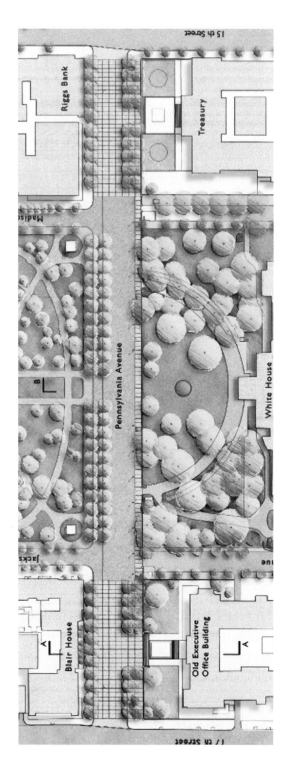

Concept design for Pennsylvania Avenue in front of the White House closed.

120

- The concept allows for secure public access to the White House precinct and President's Park through the proposed Circulator. A Circulator would permit a partial and limited use of Pennsylvania Avenue to allow for controlled and secure vehicular traffic in front of the White House. A Circulator would also help mitigate the closure of Pennsylvania Avenue by restoring a cross-town transportation link and, once more, offer to both visitors and residents the experience of riding in front of the White House. An allée of large trees delineates the route for the Circulator and defines and humanizes the space in front of the White House. The design includes a simple array of historic Washington light fixtures, stone benches, and discreet bollards.

The design concept addresses the functional requirements of security, circulation, the inaugural parade, and pedestrian amenities in the following ways:

- *Security.* The security perimeter is in the same location as the existing temporary security barriers. Inside the perimeter, no additional vehicular security is required. Security elements consist of a row of bollards located at each end of the avenue inside the 15th and 17th Street intersections. Guard booths are proposed to be located within the tree bosques. The ultimate design and location of these security elements will change as required to meet criteria established by the U.S. Secret Service and other law enforcement agencies.
- *Circulation.* The design accommodates the planned Circulator by including a travel lane for controlled and secure vehicular traffic in front of the White House. As proposed, vehicles entering the avenue will either be turned away or cleared to proceed through the perimeter barrier at the entrance to the street on the north side of Pennsylvania Avenue. This street is delineated by a shallow curb and a second row of trees that parallel the existing street trees on the south side of Lafayette Park. Whereas the Circulator will remain on this street, presidential motorcades, VIPs, law enforcement, and other authorized vehicles would cross the central pedestrian area to enter the ceremonial drive of the White House.
- *Inaugural Parade.* A 60-foot-wide uninterrupted right-of-way is maintained throughout the length of Pennsylvania Avenue between 15th and 17th Streets, as required for the Inaugural

Allée of trees shows circulator route.

Proposed streetscape looking east on Pennsylvania Avenue.

Parade. The total width of the central area in front of the White House is 90 feet, including the 15-foot sidewalk on the south, but excluding the 24-foot vehicular street on the north. Temporary bleachers that are able to seat approximately 21,000 spectators will line both sides of this route. (Temporary bleachers for the 2001 Inaugural Parade accommodated 17,500 spectators.)

- *Site Amenities.* As proposed, the entry plazas facing the Eisenhower Executive Office Building and the Treasury Building will be constructed with monolithic 10 × 15-foot slabs of granite. The central area in front of the White House will be constructed of crushed granite. Bench seating will be located in shaded areas under the trees. A simple order of historic Washington light fixtures, stone benches, and bollards chosen for their timeless appearance will reinforce the existing overall sense of the avenue.

White House street furnishings and view.

## ADDITIONAL DESIGN CONSIDERATIONS

- The design concept offers a conceptual starting point for the permanent design of Pennsylvania Avenue in front of the White House. The extraordinary historic, symbolic, and security concerns of this area will require modification and refinement as the design proceeds.
- The design and location of security elements will be modified, as necessary, to meet the criteria established by the U.S. Secret Service and other law enforcement agencies.
- The design may require modification to meet the unique requirements of the Inaugural Parade, including presidential viewing, media stands, and bleachers.

- The design must ensure that the avenue can be quickly and easily reopened to normal vehicular traffic.
- A contingency plan should be prepared to ensure that construction does not impact the Inaugural Parade. Ideally, construction should be completed in time for the 2005 parade.
- The design should not preclude the ability to incorporate a tunnel in the future, if deemed necessary and appropriate at this location.

## Symbolically Important Views, Buildings, and Gathering Areas: City Hall Park, New York City[4]

### HISTORY

The area of today's City Hall Park played an important civic role throughout New York City's history. In the mid-1650s, it was known as the *Commons* and was used as a communal pasture for livestock. In 1663, the first structure, a windmill, was constructed on the site. The windmill was later to be included as part of the City's official seal. As New York City grew, the Commons became the site of an almshouse to help impoverished city residents. In the mid-1700s, the British built the Soldier's Barracks on the north side of the Commons, the site now occupied by the Tweed Courthouse. The Commons became the site of many pre-Revolutionary protests. The Commons became the British Army's headquarters during the Revolutionary War. General George Washington led the Continental Army back into the city after the British evacuated on November 25, 1783. An American flag was raised over the Commons, and New York City served as this nation's first capital for the following seven years.

In 1803, construction began on City Hall. It was completed in 1812. The building was set back in the gated park setting. Although initially some thought the site was too far north, over time the area around City Hall was the site of many civic structures. In 1842, the Croton Fountain was built at the southern tip of the park to commemorate the building of the Croton Aqueduct. This amazing engineering feat brought the City its first dependable supply of drinking water from the Croton Dam more than 40 miles north of the city. Connected directly to the aqueduct, the Croton Fountain shot a spire of water an impressive 50 feet into the air. The Croton Fountain was replaced by the construction of a Federal Post Office. A replacement fountain was built closer to City Hall. In 1939, the Federal Post Office was torn down in anticipation of a planned restoration of the Park.

---

[4]City of New York Parks and Recreation, George Vellonakis—City Hall Park Designer.

The fountain, which had become a centerpiece of the Park, was disassembled several years earlier. However, the planned restoration of the Park was never completed, and over the years the Park gradually deteriorated from neglect.

The most recent renovation of City Hall Park was begun in the 1990s. It restored much of the park's original geometry and detail. The original granite base of the 1871 fountain was reinstalled, with the rest of the fountain and its features reconstructed from the original design. An original section of the park's wrought iron fence was found and served as a model for the new fence. The faithful historic restoration of City Hall Park was performed with an eye toward meeting the need for enhanced security of the 1990s.

## CONDITION AND CONTEXT BEFORE RESTORATION

Prior to the new design of City Hall Park, the area directly in front of City Hall was dedicated to parking. From Broadway on the west side to Park Row on the east, the entire front of City

There were no vehicular or pedestrian controls at the major entries into City Hall Park. Courtesy of George Vellonakis.

View looking south along Park Row, the eastern side of City Hall Park. Courtesy of George Vellonakis.

Hall was one big parking lot. Other than a police officer standing at each of these entrances, there were no physical barriers to prevent cars from driving right up to the front steps of City Hall. There were no pedestrian restrictions in place anywhere in the Park. The numerous entry points were not gated but merely breaks in the fence. Pedestrians were free to walk around all sides of City Hall unimpeded, and the front steps of City Hall were very often the site of impromptu news conferences concerning city issues.

View looking north along Broadway, the western side of City Hall Park. Courtesy of George Vellonakis.

The perimeter fence, as well as the fence lining the interior pedestrian walks, was a rather uninspiring piperail type, more fitting of a factory or warehouse than an important civic space. The pavement throughout the park had become uneven, with many patches incorporated into the traditional asphaltic block hexagonal pavers. The planted areas had deteriorated and looked unkept. Overall, City Hall Park had become a rather dismal setting for the centerpiece of government of one of the greatest cities in the world.

Interior view of the park showing deterioration of many of the site elements over the years. Courtesy of George Vellonakis.

The climate for the design of civic buildings and spaces had begun to change in the 1990s. In other parts of the world, American interests had been attacked by terrorists. The first bombing of the World Trade Center in 1993 and the bombing of the Murrah Federal Building in Oklahoma City brought the threat of terrorist acts to this nation's own soil. The security measures usually incorporated into foreign embassies and military bases began to be part of the design development approach for government buildings here in this country. With growing awareness and concern that terrorists could strike close to home, the design objectives of government buildings and civic spaces were overlaid with the criteria to enhance security.

## SECURITY DESIGN ELEMENTS OF THE NEW DESIGN

The design of City Hall Park is a masterful example of a faithful restoration of a historic open space, in an aesthetically beautiful way, maintaining the day-to-day government functions that take place in City Hall, while addressing the security concerns of the times in which we live. The restoration of City Hall Park proves that you do not have to choose between design excellence and security. They are goals that can be joined together creatively and compatibly.

The new design limits the physical space dedicated to the parking of vehicles in front of City Hall. There is limited parking provided to the east and west of the building, and parking directly in front of City Hall has been eliminated. This makes a tremendous improvement aesthetically, opening up magnificent views of the building from the park. Controlling vehicular access to this area and restricting those cars that are authorized to park,

Vehicular access from Broadway is restricted by a fence with a large double gate and the formidable rising vehicular barrier.

Access from Park Row is similar to the Broadway side. Visitors to City Hall must enter here and pass through a magnetometer before entering the building.

A pedestrian gate adjacent to the vehicular gate on the Broadway side allows visitors to enter after having credentials screened by the guard in the booth. The guard booth is designed in an architectural style similar to City Hall itself.

improve security by creating an adequate setback for City Hall. Access by unauthorized vehicles has been effectively eliminated.

There are vehicular entry points on both the east and west side of City Hall. Vehicular access is controlled by both steel gates and a rising vehicle barrier. The gates are electronically opened by the guard in the booth to allow authorized vehicles into the area. In the same manner, the guard lowers the vehicular barrier to allow a vehicle access. Both these barriers together provide a high level of security from unauthorized vehicular entry.

Pedestrian entry points to the area in front of City Hall are pedestrian-sized gates (adjacent to the vehicular entry points) that are usually left in the open position for authorized people to enter the area in front of City Hall. Identifications are checked, and authorized people are allowed to continue on to City Hall. There is no authorized direct access from City Hall Park to City Hall. All visitors must pass through a magnetometer before entering City Hall itself.

In an example of how the human element and procedural loophole can circumvent a well-planned physical security design, despite the high security at City Hall, a man was able to bring a gun into the City Council Chambers and shoot and kill a councilperson in 2003. As the facts of the incident were made clear, apparently the councilperson who was shot brought this person into City Hall through the staff entrance. Prior to this incident, staff who regularly worked in City Hall were not required to pass through the magnetometer. Apparently in this case, this person avoided having to be checked because he was a guest of the councilperson. This procedural gap was immediately plugged by a new order that now requires everyone, including the mayor, to pass through the magnetometer prior to entering City Hall.

The guard booths themselves are designed in keeping with the 1800s style of City Hall and fit in very nicely with the building as well as all the rest of the site amenities that carry this historical theme throughout the park. They are positioned behind the vehicular barriers, giving them an added degree of security. There is another enclosure nearby that contains the magnetometer through which all who enter City Hall—staff, visitor, or mayor—must pass.

Visitors then must be screened through a magnetometer located adjacent to the park, in front of City Hall.

The entire perimeter of City Hall Park is protected with a solid steel fence mounted in a high stone curb. The fence is designed in a style that is consistent with the architecture of City Hall itself. It is one of the elements that relates historically back to the time when City Hall was built. The granite curb is a material that is found quite commonly in New York City and is very much in keeping with the granite curbs used extensively throughout the city.

From the security perspective, the high curb is a deterrent to vehicles that might try to drive over it and through the fence. The curb is mounted on a continuous-grade beam that anchors it in place and helps the individual pieces of stone react more monolithically to an impact. Each of the fence posts are anchored into the curb but are also braced diagonally. This diagonal bracing helps each post resist any force applied to it. Each fence panel is not only attached to a post on each end but is also attached mid-panel to the stone curb with a steel connection from the bottom horizontal rail. This mid-panel connection adds valuable strength at the point where the fence might be considered weakest.

Installation of granite curb on supporting concrete, continuous-grade beam. Courtesy of George Vellonakis.

Fence installed in granite curb with diagonal bracing at posts and midpanel connection to curb.

Midpanel connection to granite curb adds strength.

The decorative columns that are located at each of the major vehicular entry points, as well as at the major entrance on the southern end of the park, are heavily reinforced. Although they look to be comprised of individual masonry units mortared together, a typical construction technique, they are instead a monolithic casting. The column itself is hollow and has been installed over a concrete pipe filled with concrete that is anchored firmly in place. This adds a great deal of strength to the

Southern entrance with retractable bollards and double gate with views of the fountain provide inviting access to City Hall Park.

Decorative columns installed over securely anchored metal pipe with retractable bollards flank the large double-gate southern entrance.

areas around potential vehicular access points that helps bolster the fence and gate structure to any impacts.

The other pedestrian entrances to the park are larger openings designed with double gates that can be closed if necessary. In front of each of these pedestrian access points are retractable bollards that are generally left in the raised position. They allow unimpeded public pedestrian access to the park, yet at the same time serve as an effective barrier to any vehicles that might attempt entry into the park through these openings.

The simplicity and effectiveness that this design represents was very much evident on the morning of 9/11. In a relatively short time, City Hall and City Hall Park were locked down by existing security personnel by simply closing and locking the gates. As time passed and the immediate threat lessened, the gates were able to be opened again, and the park was returned to the vibrant, civic space it had been before the attacks. This serves as an excellent example of how good, permanent security design can be responsive in times of heightened alert and flexible enough to respond as changing circumstances might warrant.

Access to City Hall Park can be restricted to the public simply by closing and locking the gates. Courtesy of George Vellonakis.

The security design is flexible, so that City Hall Park can be made accessible to the public as changing circumstances warrant, simply by opening the gates.

Another excellent strategy employed in the design of City Hall Park is the placement of the centrally located fountain, site amenities, and planting beds. The location of these elements prevents a straight-line access to the front of City Hall. Any vehicle that might gain entry—even a motorcycle or scooter—would need to slow down to divert around these obstacles, slowing the intruder and giving security personnel valuable extra time to act. At the same time, all these elements, benches, lightpoles, trash receptacles and particularly the fountain, are designed in a style that harkens back to the days of early New York and are very much in keeping with the historical context of City Hall and the surrounding area.

Aerial view of City Hall Park showing location of various site elements. Courtesy of George Vellonakis.

Planter beds and centrally located fountain help control circulation routes within the park.

Benches, trash receptacles, interior bollards, and chains reflect the character of City Hall.

Traditional light standard used in City Hall Park.

"Bishop's crook" harkens back to an early time in the city's history.

A central feature of the park's redesign is the reconstruction, of the original fountain, including gas lights.

Close-up of gas lights that evoke the history of New York City and City Hall Park.

Historical information is conveyed by this interpretive pavement detail located on the southern end of the park.

Completing the historical theme of the park are a variety of pavement etchings with photos and information detailing a period of New York City's history. These interpretive paving features provide interesting historical facts for both visitors and New Yorkers. The ambience of the overall design and character of the site elements add to the experience of those enjoying the park and the area around it. At the same time, it is a design that enhances security in a virtually transparent manner while enriching the experience of pedestrian and visitor.

The security design features in City Hall Park enhance the stature and dignity of this important civic building and the access to the beautiful public open space it is situated in.

## Local Government: California State House, Sacramento[5]

Balancing security design with an appearance representative of an open and democratic society is a concern at the state level. In many ways, the increased security at state capitol buildings are similar to the efforts at the Capitol in Washington, D.C. In the wake of 9/11, many states increased the numbers of security personnel, surveillance cameras, metal detectors, and barricades of various types. Since that time, some states have begun to roll back their levels of security to levels that they have determined to be more in line with the assessed risk.

The Capitol building in Sacramento was a picture of an openness of government represented by a site design that had no fences or other types of barriers. An original fence and bollards were originally installed at the Capitol but they were removed and melted down to aid in the war effort during the 1940s. Security concerns rose after the Oklahoma City terrorist bombing. In response, then Governor Pete Wilson proposed building a low wall with a wrought iron fence around the perimeter of the Capitol grounds. The plan met with a good deal of opposition, and there was discussion regarding the historic and aesthetic impact such a barrier would have. An environmental impact report on the Wilson plan raised some safety concerns, as well, one being the possibility of an event at one of the frequent demonstration creating a scenario that would require large numbers of people to have to exit the Capitol grounds quickly. The proposed perimeter fence would impede their ability to leave the area. There was also concern that the fence would make access by emergency vehicles more difficult, resulting in a delayed response. During this period of the mid-1990s, these negative impacts were judged to be a greater safety concern than someone attacking the Capitol with a car bomb.

However, that all changed in 2001. In January of that year, a mentally disturbed individual crashed a tractor trailer truck into the Capitol building. After circling the Capitol several times, the

---

[5]The HLA Group, Sacramento, California.

Freestanding planters are too small to offer any real security against a vehicle that could easily make its way through.

Freestanding planters provide little real security.

Precast concrete barriers provide an additional level of security here, but the gap left adjacent to them would allow a vehicle access to the Capitol by crashing through the planters.

driver, Mike Bowers, turned his truck up 11th Street towards the Capitol and accelerated. With horn blaring, the truck raced through an intersection against the light at a speed in excess of 50 miles an hour. It jumped the curb, went across the park, up the stairs and crashed through the doors of the Capitol before bursting into flames. The truck, carrying only milk, still did extensive damage to the structure, requiring $20 million to repair, but the only loss of life was that of the driver. If this had been a terrorist act that included an explosive cargo, the resulting damage to the building and potential loss of life could have been catastrophic.

A number of temporary barriers were put in place including a number of large planters. The planters are not anchored in place and are more of a visual barrier than one that truly provides effective security against a speeding vehicle. This attack of a disgruntled and disturbed individual revived the discussion as to whether a fence and wall of the type originally proposed would have stopped such an attack. Many officials who had opposed the original proposal of a fence and wall were now supportive of constructing barriers to prevent a reoccurrence of this type of vehicular attack. The events of 9/11 later that year, strengthened their resolve to enhance the security of the Capitol. In 2002, the legislature began the process of moving forward by approving detailed construction cost estimates and soliciting proposals for enhanced security.

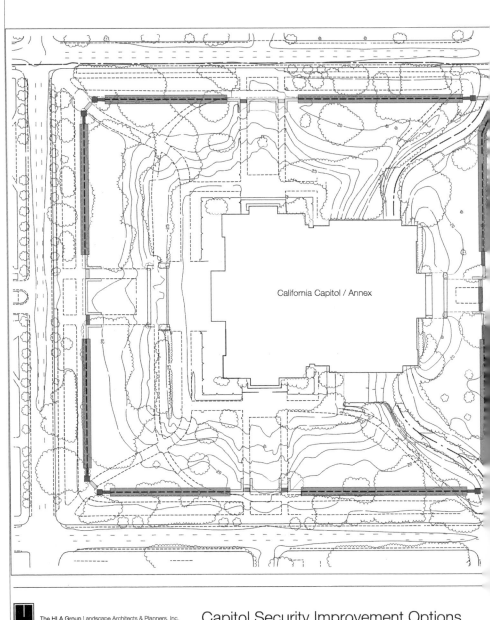

 The HLA Group Landscape Architects & Planners, Inc.
1990 Third Street, Suite 500 / Sacramento, California 95814
916.447.7400 / 916.447.8270 fax / www.hlagroup.com

## Capitol Security Improvement Options
### Perimeter Security Option 1
Sacramento, California

Proposed security design enhancements protect the Capitol without sacrificing the character of the park setting around it.

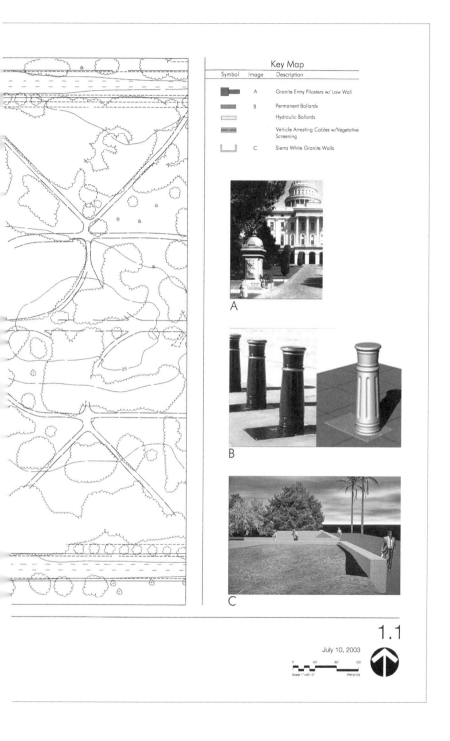

Key Map

| Symbol | Image | Description |
|---|---|---|
| | A | Granite Entry Pilasters w/ Low Wall |
| | B | Permanent Bollards |
| | | Hydraulic Bollards |
| | | Vehicle Arresting Cables w/Vegetative Screening |
| | C | Sierra White Granite Walls |

A

B

C

1.1

July 10, 2003

0    40'    80'    120'

Scale 1"=40'-0"         PN#9103

Bollards and light standards work together to prevent unauthorized vehicular entry from this corner of the Capitol grounds.

A primary concern driving the preparation of the site design proposal was the desire to minimize the aesthetic intrusion of the security elements and maximize the enhancement of security for the Capitol. This is particularly important in this instance, as the Capitol grounds are used extensively for public gatherings and demonstrations as well as a park for downtown residents and workers. There are a significant number of heritage trees and shrubs planted that add to the value of this urban open space as a *mini-arboretum*. The proposal works around these valuable plants, incorporating them into the new design.

The security design proposal calls for the perimeter of the Capitol grounds to be protected with bollards to prevent vehicular access. There are granite entry planters designed with low

Bollards do not always have to be placed in a straight line. A curved placement provides security and variety.

walls at the primary pedestrian entry points. The proposals call for two visitor pavilions that will allow for the screening and queuing of those entering the Capitol. The use of bollards, similar to those used at the Capitol in Washington, D.C., are a primary component of the security design response. They provide

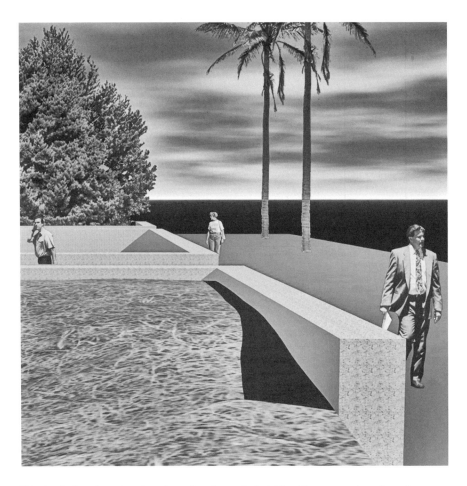

This visualization shows how berming soil on the protected side of the proposed granite walls can lessen the visual impact on the park side yet project a vision of a strong physical barrier to the vehicular side.

for the desired vehicular restriction and at the same time give the Capitol grounds the desired open feel. Hydraulically operated retractable bollards provide access for emergency and maintenance vehicles.

In addition to the traditional bollard response, there are unique security design elements, details, and strategies proposed that deserve attention. One such detail is the treatment of the low granite walls. This element is an effective barrier and an attractive element very much in keeping with the dignified look of the Capitol itself. In order to soften the impact of the wall and add variety to the pedestrian experience, the proposal changes

In addition to minimizing the impact of the walls from the park view, the additional soil behind the walls adds to their impact resistance.

the grade to rise toward the top of the wall on the protected side. This gesture minimizes the visual impact of the wall to those within the park but still presents its full height and expression as a formidable barrier to those outside the park, especially vehicles. The soil that rises behind the wall adds extra resistance, making it more effective as a vehicular barrier than a free-standing wall without this topography change.

Installation of bollards along the pathways of the park protect without damaging the experience of the visitor.

The use of steel vehicle arresting cables within the vegetation provides an alternative to long runs of bollards. The approach of not relying on a single element provides variety and rhythm along these long linear paths.

Another unique detail is the use of tensioned steel cables screened with vegetation to provide unauthorized vehicular entry. The steel cable effectively prevents vehicles from passing through, yet at the same time enhances the park-like feel of the Capitol grounds. It is used in conjunction with the low granite walls and bollards to provide enhanced security. It is a good example of how a variety of different elements can be combined in a security design response rather than relying on any single element.

Overall, the security design for the Capitol in Sacramento is a measured response balanced against the assessed risk, which actually includes a pre-9/11 act of domestic terrorism. Interestingly, original opposition to any constructed barriers prior to that incident evolved into a more thoughtful permanent security design solution that addresses the role of the Capitol grounds as an integral, urban open space for downtown Sacramento.

# Office Buildings and Public Space: Site Security Design and Collaborative Management, Ronald Reagan/International Trade Center Building, Washington, D.C.[6]

The Reagan/ITC Building is an extraordinary federal building in many respects, not the least of which is the sheer amount of public activity that occurs there. The building includes a food court, restaurant, and the official District of Columbia visitors' center, all open to the public; offices for federal agencies and private businesses; and conference and meeting facilities where nearly 1,200 events—from a summit of ministers from NATO nations to trade forums to weddings—are held each year. Woodrow Wilson Plaza/Daniel Patrick Moynihan Place, just outside, hosts a daily lunchtime performance series in the summer, as well as special events like Hollywood-style film premieres and cooking extravaganzas.

Ironically, this busy 3.1-million-square-foot building is located in the heart of the largest federal office compound in the country—the seven-square-block Federal Triangle. For the most part, it is a quiet area, wedged between the bustle of Washington's downtown retail district and the tourist-thronged attractions on the Mall. Except for the National Archives and Old Post Office Building a few blocks down Pennsylvania Avenue, there are no major public facilities nearby.

The diverse activities in the Reagan/ITC Building (the second largest federal office building, after the Pentagon) are not only an exemplar of GSA's Good Neighbor policies, but also an important part of the building's finances. Unlike most federal buildings, its construction was funded via long-term debt, and the ITC (the public component) receives no annual operating appropri-

[6]Bressi, Todd, *Before the Jersey Barrier: Public Access and Public Safety in Federal Buildings.* Used with permission of the author, Todd Bressi, and the permission of the U.S. General Services Administration.

ation. Rents from federal tenants and revenues from ITC operations (rents from private sector tenants and fees for special
events) help retire the debt and also contribute toward the management and operating costs of the building.

Security concerns have always been paramount here,
because of the building's location (on Pennsylvania Avenue
between the White House and the Capital), because the building
was opened after the Murrah bombing, and due to the high con-
centration of federal workers in the building (which houses the
headquarters of the U.S. Customs Service, the U.S. Agency for
International Development, and the Woodrow Wilson
International Center for Scholars, as well as a component of the
Environmental Protection Agency). GSA's Federal Protective
Service (FPS) and the manager of the Trade Center's public
spaces and events have evolved an in-depth, yet straightforward,
protocol for maintaining necessary security while allowing all
manner of public activities.

Security occurs in layers. Since the building is nestled in the
Federal Triangle compound, only two sides are open to the
street, and vehicles are made to keep their distance by on-street
parking restrictions and bollards that prevent access to the plaza.
GSA has a more attractive perimeter security concept plan that
will provide the necessary security while making it more visually appealing and accessible on a human scale.

The guards (who are also a GSA contractor force) who are at
the building's seven entrances and security cameras that monitor the streets and entrances "are our security perimeter. They
are like a fence, just an invisible fence," explains Douglas Avery,
GSA's Deputy Security Manager for the building. Anybody can
stroll into the plaza or walk into Michael Jordan's restaurant,
which is tucked into a pavilion on one side of the Reagan/ITC
Building, without passing through any special checkpoint. To get
into the building's public spaces, though, visitors must pass
through an airport-style checkpoint. And to enter one of the
towers that houses federal and private offices, visitors must pass
through a second, airport-style screening.

This system provides a base level of security for the entire
building while allowing the federal agencies to tailor additional

levels of inspection to their own needs, Avery says. "To a person not used to security, it can be disconcerting, but once inside, you can walk anywhere," says Don Shapiro, who manages events and security for the trade center manager.

Deliveries are carefully choreographed by the FPS, the guard service contractor, and the trade center manager, the latter of whom also oversees the garage operations. Delivery trucks must be screened off-site, at the Southeast Federal Center, then sealed for the trip downtown. Then, when the trucks park at the loading dock, someone must stay with them at all times. In addition, the trade center manager does all catering in-house and has developed a list of preferred vendors for other services; the manager collects background information about his employees and sends it to FPS for review and approval.

"It's not taking the easiest route; efficiency is not the first thing we look at here," Shapiro acknowledges. "But once you follow the procedure, it's easy, and there's no delay." While it may add a bit to the cost of doing business at the ITC, many clients think the trade-off is fair for the level of security the building offers, he adds.

In practice, the key to making these arrangements work has been flexibility. The trade center manager and FPS have weekly planning meetings, and the building's security committee convenes biweekly, so there is plenty of opportunity to anticipate and address special situations. "We do try to balance security needs with the building's legislative mission to be open and accessible to the public," Avery says. Shapiro agrees: "There's lots of give and take."

For example, one client requested a reception that would take place both in the building's atrium and under a tent on the plaza. To accomplish this, guests were screened at the building entrance and given a special wristband, which allowed them to move out to the plaza and back inside. The plaza area was configured with a secure perimeter, which was patrolled by guards hired especially for the event and paid for by the client.

Another event involved so many guests that they could not be screened efficiently at the building entrance. So the event sponsor asked guests to assemble at a different location, where they were screened and put on buses, which were escorted to the building.

Like many federal buildings post–September 11, "this place was a fortress," Avery says. Everyone entering the building was screened, with the result that "people were lined up to Virginia just to get inside, and that was not acceptable." But because the building had such thorough procedures in place, it could get back to normal in short order. The parking garage was closed for only two days, and a wedding went on as scheduled the very next weekend.

Business dropped off briefly last fall, but over the 12 months, business has been stronger than it was in the previous year— despite a general decline in the hospitality business in Washington in the same period. This is a tribute both to the popularity of the building and to the spirit of flexibility and partnership in which GSA's management and contractors operate.

# Programming and Public–Private Collaboration in Site Security: The Hanley Federal Building and U.S. Courthouse, Syracuse, New York[7]

The "Party in the Plaza" at the Hanley Federal Building and U.S. Courthouse is more than a 19-year tradition; it's a lynchpin of nightlife in Syracuse, New York. Every Wednesday in the summer, starting at about 5 P.M., the party fills up the plaza that surrounds the courthouse/office complex, even flowing underneath an elevated section of the building. Up to 10,000 people turn out to listen to bands, dance, and munch on all manner of festival food.

"This makes or breaks businesses in downtown Syracuse; it's like another weekend night," explains William A. Cooper, president of the UpDowntowners, the volunteer group that organizes the events. On top of that, profits are distributed among other local groups to help them organize additional public events downtown—last year, 15 groups split $48,000.

Security for the event was tightened after the Oklahoma City bombing, according to Cooper and Joan Grennan, the GSA's property manager for the building. Since then, for example, city police and bomb-sniffing dogs have inspected every vehicle that comes on the plaza—including delivery trucks, trailers for food vendors, and even the local radio station's promotional van.

"This year, though, we had some increased concerns," Grennan says. "The chief judge invited us in to see if this should be a 'go' or a 'no go.' He was interested in hearing what additional security measures they were going to provide." Relocation wasn't an option; no other downtown public space had the right

---

[7]Used with permission of the author, Todd Bressi, and the permission of the U.S. General Services Administration.

configuration or facilities. So the UpDowntowners, in conjunction with GSA, the FPS, the chief judge, and the U.S. Marshals (who oversee security for courts), mapped out additional security measures.

One step was to bolster the presence of security officers. More than a dozen uniformed city police are on the scene, as well as FPS officers and contract security (the UpDowntowners pick up the extra cost). Security risks were reduced by moving portable toilets and dumpsters farther from the building and by banning parking on streets surrounding the plaza during events.

Partygoers have had to get used to a new ban on backpacks at the event. Security staff observe everybody who enters the site, which has four access points, but there are no metal detectors or searches. "We don't stop everyone, we do visual checks. When we see people with a backpack, we go over and ask them not to bring it onto the premises," Cooper says.

Finally, the UpDowntowners increased the number of volunteers who mingle with the crowd and provided them all with special antiterrorist training. Under the guidance of a retired Army officer, "we review what to look for in terms of suspects, terrorists, and suspicious characters," Cooper explains.

Complaints about the new arrangements have been minimal, according to Cooper. "The security is not obvious. Some people complain that they've come on the bus and have no place to put their backpacks. But most people drive, and they can leave it in their cars."

A key reason these arrangements could be effective is UpDowntowners' solid track record of collaborating with the GSA and building tenants. "As part of their planning every year, they put together a proposal about the organization, their licenses, [and] their insurance," says Grennan, "and they would talk to every judge in the building and a lot of politicians, and get their blessings, in letter form, for us."

Another reason is that the event was too important for Syracuse to cancel. "When it started, there was a beat-up slum section a few blocks away," Grennan recalls. "Now that area has come back, with boutiques and bars, and those places advertise in the paper to come see them after the party. This has brought the area up."

No argument from Cooper: "This is a good thing for the federal government. It says, 'We're not being held hostage due to threats. We are taking precautions, but we are doing business as usual.' "

# Conclusion

Prior to 9/11, there was little thought given to physical security in the United States. Now we know better.

Terrorist groups can be large or small, highly centralized, or loosely linked. The rising awareness of the diversity and number of terrorist groups compounds this problem. It is questionable whether a successful attack against the leader of one of these groups would cause the group to fall apart or give up terrorist actions for their cause. The best protection against this type of threat is good intelligence, surveillance, and infiltration of these groups to prevent attacks while still in the planning stages before the attacks take place. The next level of defense is physical barriers and detection technologies—both effective countermeasures that can serve as strong deterrents preventing attacks from taking place or minimizing the loss of life and property.

The range of threats includes small arms weapons; larger-scale weapons like antitank weapons, shoulder-held missile launchers, and mortars; Molotov cocktails; bombs; and a variety of chemical, biological, and radiological agents. These weapons can be sent through the mail; strategically placed in locations for detonation; planted in parked or moving vehicles; or delivered by individuals. The size of bomb that can be used depends on the ability of the delivery means to carry the explosives. A bomb-laden truck or vehicle can carry enough blast potential to bring down a building. A bomb strapped to an individual or a backpack has less of an ability to cause such widespread damage and loss of life. Good security design must protect against these various weapons and different levels of threat in an approach that prioritizes the deterrent against the most damaging types of terrorist acts.

## TRADITIONAL BARRIERS

As attention turns toward considering how we could replace the temporary barriers erected with good, permanent security design, our immediate attention had been given to the use of traditional barrier elements. In cases where the highest level of security is required, particularly where buildings are designed with vehicular entry points, heavy-duty fence and locking gates, rising vehicular barriers, beam barriers, and guard booths are still required. However, even these extreme measures to address security can be done in a manner consistent with good design principles. Parking barriers need to work together with adequate thought given to their layout, allowing cars to queue without impeding pedestrian travel on the sidewalk or disrupting vehicle flow on the street, along with a secure guard booth that is complementary to the architecture of the building and the surrounding area.

To secure the perimeter of the site, bollards were one of the most popular site elements. They are available in a wide range of styles, colors, and sizes, and come in retractable models to secure the perimeter but allow maintenance and emergency vehicle access when necessary. However, the proliferation of the bollard lining the sidewalk along the street, as if it were the only site element available to provide perimeter security, takes away from its effectiveness as an aesthetically pleasing design element. Unfortunately, the bollard has become such a common response to perimeter security that its overuse diminishes its design value. Its overuse has resulted in a design response that often seems an automatic response, in a cookie-cutter approach, that overlooks other options available to protect the site.

In much the same way, the permanent raised planters that were used to replace temporary barriers were installed without being given a high level of design thought or detailing. Often used to replace the large, temporary, freestanding concrete planters—or *bunker pots*—in many cases, they offered little improvement as a single design element over the temporary measures they replaced.

## IMPROVED SITE AMENITIES

Today, there is an increased understanding that the first step in planning for enhanced security is to perform an accurate and realistic risk assessment of a facility's threat level before considering the appropriate design response for meeting that threat. This important step is often overlooked, as there is a tendency to overdesign or create unnecessary redundancies in a security design response. Not every facility or building requires the same level of protection against potential terrorist activities. Permanent security design is currently focused on employing a variety of site amenities, using a broad spectrum of landscape architectural strategies and techniques to enhance security as well as create a rich streetscape for pedestrians.

Current federal policy and guidelines allow for varying levels of physical responses to the various levels of potential threat. Buildings requiring the highest levels of protection—because of threats and potential high-speed, unimpeded perpendicular vehicular access—still require the highest (and usually most visible) physical security elements. However, buildings with a lower level of risk can be adequately protected with a much wider array of site elements that have the positive impact of enriching the streetscape while providing the appropriate level of security.

Site amenities that can be creatively used to provide perimeter security (lest we become cities of bollards) include major trees with tree guards, benches, planters, bike racks, information kiosks, bus shelters, overhead structures, signage, and flagpoles. These are among the more common elements used to provide vehicular barriers along the street and effective perimeter security.

Building plazas and public gathering places can also use raised planters, changes in elevation (i.e., steps, ramps, and railings), walls, fences, colonnades, statues, and fountains. All of these site amenities can enhance and complement the character of an area and architecture of adjacent buildings, as well as provide a meaningful reason for widening pedestrian sidewalks.

Landscape architects have all used these familiar design techniques before, and they can be used again strategically to enhance security. This security enhancement will safely allow people to gather in our public and civic spaces, taking part in a wide variety of positive activities. These gatherings are an important part of who we are as a nation, and we must not let security concerns prevent us from coming together.

Each of these elements can be beautifully designed and carefully sited such that their commonplace, everyday character disguises their protective role. However, the most successful implementations consist of many elements combined together rather than instead of any one element. One should think of the vocabulary of site amenities as separate threads woven to create a rich fabric. This can be achieved by using familiar site elements while providing effective security in a seamless, transparent manner.

The use of these traditional nonsecurity elements allows a great deal of flexibility and creativity in a design response. One strategy in addressing the need to stop vehicles from speeding toward a facility is to not provide those vehicles a straight path by which they can accelerate to dangerous speeds. Carefully locating elements and changes in grade are extremely effective in preventing vehicles from attaining speeds requiring more extreme security measures. This approach then provides the opportunity to employ a broader spectrum of common site elements that can withstand the impact of slower moving vehicles.

## NEED FOR IMPACT STANDARDS

In the future, landscape architects would benefit from specification drawings and materials specifications for *hardened* site furnishings. These standards would be a valuable reference for developing new site security designs. Currently, a number of different standards are being employed by various federal agencies. A unified federal standard that could be referenced by state and local governments, as well as corporate and private owners, would help design professionals meet applicable security levels with a greater deal of certainty.

As part of this initiative, necessary testing and data need to be made available to design practitioners, making it easier to determine a product's ability to meet vehicular impact criteria and establish necessary anchoring requirements. Nontraditional site amenities that provide perimeter and site security, such as flagpoles, tree guards, and park benches, do not currently come with data relating to their ability to withstand impacts. Many site amenity manufacturers are now developing products to be integrated into a security design response, but a government-certified rating is not normally applied.

At this point in time, the success of many site security installations is tested on a case-by-case basis. Before they can be used to enhance security, they must be modified or hardened to resist vehicular impacts. This may involve strengthening the element by increasing the size or strength of its components, or the way those components are connected. It most certainly would involve strengthening the manner in which these elements are usually anchored in place. If this information could be made available in a standardized format that related to national security design criteria, it would help design professionals be more creative in the design development of physical security enhancements.

A great deal of a site element's ability to withstand an impact is at the point of connection to the pavement, curb, or footing. The size of curbs or footings may have to be increased to withstand vehicular impact. An element that might usually be anchored in a footing of concrete typically one foot square by three feet deep might now require a footing three or four feet square by five feet deep. Site features typically anchored in a footing might even require modification for anchoring in a substantial underground-grade beam to create a more monolithic resistance to impact. Most of these hardening techniques are invisible to the casual observer, hence the value of using commonplace site amenities to enhance security. However, special considerations are necessary because of the substantial below-grade modifications. The areas typically benefiting from the use of these amenities as security measures, particularly the sidewalk to the curb line, often have underground utilities running beneath them, installed at a depth not conducive to this type of construction. As such, conflicts with underground utilities need to be studied before embarking on a security design effort of this type.

Additionally, the increased size of underground footings, curbs, and grade beams can have disastrous effects on existing trees, and can severely limit the development or lifespan of newly planted ones. Damage to the root structure of existing trees should be minimized, and new trees should be given ample opportunity for their roots to spread. The use of structural soils to provide both a positive growing environment for tree roots and the integrity to support pavements above should be considered. This type of streetscape improvement for security purposes often requires the removal of sidewalk pavement. As we move forward, the opportunity to maximize a tree's ability to survive the urban environment while performing as a security element should not be missed. The location of underground utility lines and tree roots is so critical that, in some cases, it drives the location and even feasibility of streetscape elements for enhanced perimeter security.

## COHESIVENESS OF SECURITY MEASURES

As it is likely that there will be more permanent security designs implemented, there must be some consideration regarding overall impact of perimeter security measures. We need to ask ourselves, "What if everyone did that?" Good security design should be something that can be added to in a manner that will produce continuity and cohesiveness for the urban streetscape. Another consideration is the protection of a building midblock when

**Figure 5-1**
Midblock barriers in the sidewalk can restrict pedestrian circulation and be disruptive to the streetscape environment. Courtesy Ted Wolff.

there are no other security measures on the adjacent properties. In some cases, this is leading to barriers being erected in the sidewalk to stop unauthorized vehicles that can gain access to the sidewalk from further down the street. (See Figure 5-1). This approach can be very disruptive to pedestrian movement on the sidewalk. A better way to approach this scenario would be to implement a unified perimeter security design for the entire street, recognizing that some buildings may need this level of protection even though others may not. By considering the security needs of the entire block holistically, an appropriate security response can be developed that will eliminate the need for mid-sidewalk barriers that can impede pedestrian circulation.

As part of this effort to look at the overall impact of security design measures comprehensively, we should begin to think about developing design guidelines that will provide a framework for the implementation of future security design measures. The establishment of such a set of guidelines could help set a standard for security design that could contribute to an organized (not standardized) approach as we address these concerns in the future. As we move further from the events of 9/11, there is a lessening of priority and urgency to implement necessary security measures. Other issues begin to compete in priority, and that can compromise the effectiveness of a security response. Guidelines established while our focus and resolve are high can ensure that we do not become complacent in the future.

## THE FUTURE OF SECURITY AND SITE DESIGN

Our security designs should be forward looking and plan for new threats and new technologies in our designs. This may mean approaching security design improvements as part of a phased implementation, with greater detail and fine-tuning at each phase of the effort. Given constraints of funds and timing, priorities must be set based on the probability of certain types of attacks, against certain targets, in certain locations. Although the criteria are somewhat subjective, nonetheless they must be applied to prioritize security implementations within the constraints of available resources.

Designs that define and control pedestrian circulation, not impede it, can provide opportunities for future integration of new technologies. Work is progressing on sensor technologies to identify a broad spectrum of threats. Devices produced for the military for battlefield detection of biological, chemical, and radiological weapons provide a good starting point. In order for these sensors to be effective, they will need to identify a broad spectrum of threats with a high degree of accuracy and minimal false readings. Currently, the best way to accomplish this is through the use of trained dogs. Scientists are working to unlock the key to what underlies these dogs' ability to detect and identify such a wide range of different chemicals. Biological sensors that can identify the organism and molecular make-up of a biological agent would complement the usual practices of tracking unusual increases in the number of emergency room visits of patients with similar symptoms. They may be helpful in determining a course of medical response and treatment that would be needed as quickly as possible in case of a terrorist attack. Radiological sensors employed at points of entry into the country as well as at specific potential targets can identify threatening material. Our site designs can transparently provide opportunities for these devices, when they come online, to identify threats before they enter the building.

Behavioral science is an area of study that could be better integrated into the development of security designs. Behavioral science and human factors need to be understood as a component in security design to create systems that increase the perceived risk of getting caught or failing in a terrorist act. If these factors could be integrated into a security design, the physical barriers could be complemented with a tactical psychological advantage, making the security design an even more effective deterrent. Designs can be developed that allow security personnel to easily recognize unusual or suspicious behavior or activity. Human factors integrated into a physical security design in a complementary approach can exploit weaknesses in terrorist character and provide the opportunity for security personnel to be responsive. They can be used in ways to strengthen the physical and psychological security of the general public. In a physical security design, the weakest link can sometimes be the human element. A human failure can render the entire system ineffective. We need to develop designs that take these factors into account in order to minimize the risk of human error and maximize vigilance and heightened awareness.

The close integration of societal systems (energy, communication, transportation, etc.) means that the destruction of one system affects the others. Their interdependence can result in a domino effect that can ultimately lead to a catastrophic failure of all the systems. We need to protect our energy systems, including generating plants, transmission lines, and gas and oil pipelines. Our communications systems are essential in an emergency situation, and all facilities related to their proper functioning need to be protected as part of a comprehensive security design effort. Safeguarding our transportation systems is best achieved with integrated and layered security responses. The integration of security measures ensures that operating efficiency is an important criterion in transportation systems. An immediate response would be to look for opportunities to improve on existing systems.

In transportation, a layered approach prevents the defeating of one aspect of the security system leading to the breakdown of the entire network of security defenses. The difficulty and likelihood of defeating such a layered approach can be a strong deterrent to a terrorist attack.

An example of this type of approach can be seen with air travel. Security starts with the airport design and how passengers are dropped off. Then there is the luggage handling and screening process. Another layer is the individual screening of each passenger. And finally, the aircraft itself represents a layer of security with strengthened cockpit doors and the presence of air marshals on flights. This sort of layered approach can be tailored to rail and other forms of transportation.

Security concerns have made the integration of building architecture and site design increasingly critical. The close collaboration of architect, landscape architect, and structural engineer can result in both responsive and inspirational designs. Indeed, there is a growing recognition that site security measures and design excellence need not be mutually exclusive.

However, we need to continually revisit our security responses as terrorists increase their level of technical sophistication and information on bombs and toxins becomes more readily available. Systems of information, communication, transportation, infrastructure, and government functions are so integrated that disruption of one component affects and can lead to the failure of others. This is a dynamic situation where threats may change, some lessening and others rising to higher levels of concern. Terrorists might modify their goals or change their tactics. Our nation needs to be prepared to be responsive to those changes. A characteristic of good security design must be the ability to respond quickly to changing circumstances with a depth of defenses that can be built upon, providing a foundation for countering terrorism in the future.

We are at a pivotal point. When the history of this time is finally written, it must not reflect a period of fear. Instead, it should be recognized as an era of strengthened freedom and renewed liberty. And as proof, the environment we build in response to our security concerns will reflect the values and ideals of the free and democratic society we are committed to protect and preserve.

# Epilogue

As this book goes to print, there are several projects that provide reasons for being optimistic about the way we approach security design as we move forward. These projects successfully integrate good site design principles and enhanced security measures. They are good examples of how landscape architecture and allied professions have evolved to where good security design need not be obvious or overbearing. It is very similar to the way that barrier free accessibility is now routinely integrated into our site designs, rather than something added at the end of a project to meet a regulatory requirement. Security site design can be achieved through basic landscape architectural principles that integrate security needs in a seamless and transparent way. The site design elements utilized can contribute to the meaning of the design and enhance the experience of the people that pass through the open space.

Two good examples of alternatives to the typical bollard installation to prevent vehicular access are the Irish Hunger Museum and the entry point to the New York City Financial District from Broadway, both in lower Manhattan.

The Irish Hunger Memorial, which contains stones from each of Ireland's 32 counties, is elevated on a limestone plinth. From its eastern approach the Memorial appears as a sloping landscape with a pathway, the ruins of a fieldstone cottage, a series of stone walls and the stones from Ireland highlighting the naturalistic rural landscape plantings. From this approach, large boulders placed on the sidewalk effectively block vehicular access to this area. These boulders function as an extension of the Memorial itself and are very much fitting with the theme and aesthetic of their context.

Large rocks placed at the perimeter relate to the design aesthetic of the Irish Hunger Memorial (designed by artist Brian Tolle, landscape architect Gail Wittwer-Laird) restrict vehicular access.

On November 26, 2003, the Lower Manhattan Development Corporation announced a plan to revitalize the heart of Manhattan's Financial District. The series of proposed streetscape improvements surrounding the New York Stock Exchange are described in the press release as, "intended to make the area more attractive and easier to navigate without compromising the increased security measures in place since 9/11."

As part of the first phase of those improvements, vehicular circulation was restricted at the intersection of Broadway and Wall Street which is an important gateway into the Financial District. The rich bronze finish of the installed sculptures conveys the financial dealings of this District in a visual way. They provide unimpeded pedestrian access and have also turned into a well-known landmark for meeting at lunchtime and after work. The sculptures are easily recognizable and even provide comfortable seating.

Bronze sculptures restrict vehicular access to New York's Financial District in the design by Rogers Marvel Architects with landscape architects Quennell Rothschild & Partners.

The sculptural barricades have become a popular meeting place.

The Lower Manhattan Development Corporation announcement described future phases that may include a water feature as a gesture to the 17th century Amsterdam Canal that ran down Broad Street; a wall with historical information erected on the original site of the protective wall that gave Wall Street its name; and a comprehensive series of pedestrian plaza amenities, including outdoor dining, that will transform this District into a vibrant part of Lower Manhattan's evening activity areas. The envisioned improvements provide the required level of security and at the same time improve the pedestrian experience for residents, workers and visitors.

A new innovation in site security design employs "Break-Away" ground planes to restrict vehicular access without the use of vertical elements as barriers. New York designers are now creating setbacks from buildings by using hidden ditches adjacent to roadways. Conventional streetscape elements, such as pavers, suspended planted areas, tree grates, recessed lighting, and plain street grates cover the ditches. The surface elements are strong enough to bear the weight of pedestrians, but collapse under the weight of a vehicle. These 'break away' ground plane elements

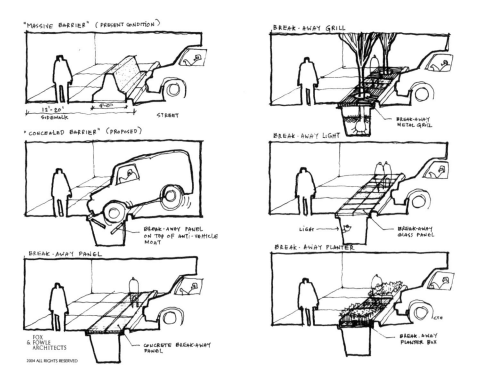

Diagrams of innovative "break-away" surface elements. Courtesy of Fox & Fowle Architects

use the weight of an attacker's vehicle to trap the car or truck in the hidden ditch.

The Smithsonian Institution's new National Museum of the American Indian, opened 2004, creatively employs site elements to implement setbacks while evoking the project's theme and providing enjoyable public spaces. The 250,000 square foot museum is located on a 4.25-acre landscaped site that includes four distinct habitats (upland hardwood forest, wetlands, meadow, agricultural area). The grounds, which include 30,000 trees, shrubs, and other plants, reveal the importance of nature in Native American culture. The museum expects to attract six million visitors a year at its site on the National Mall. The location is close to the US Capitol, prominent federal office buildings, and other nationally significant Smithsonian museums. This means the museum's site design process included pressure to satisfy the project's unique mission along with security concerns, heavy public pedestrian access, visitor experience needs, and heavy vehicular traffic on all sides.

Forty boulders are incorporated into the perimeter control system as bollards that are also usable for informal seating. The landscape treatment includes grade changes (steps, seat walls,

Boulders are combined with conventional bollards, seat walls, and raised planters to create an attractive setback that also expresses the project's theme. This significant open space was designed by a team that included Donna House (Navajo-Oneida), ethno-botanist landscape consultant; Johnpaul Jones (Cherokee-Choctaw) of Jones and Jones, design consultant; Lou Weller (Caddo-Cherokee), design consultant; EDAW, landscape architects.

and raised planters) and conventional bollards mixed with other elements to provide an interesting and attractive urban landscape that doubles as a site security design.

As mentioned in the case study section, the new design for the 1,600-foot-long pedestrian plaza along Pennsylvania Avenue between 15th and 17th streets NW in Washington, DC, intends to create a dignified, publicly accessible space on the northern boundary of the White House that enforces setbacks and restrictions for most vehicular traffic. The busy downtown roadway was closed in 1995 for security reasons. It reopened in November 2004 with the new landscape design as a pedestrian boulevard (construction and plant installation to be completed in 2005).

The design divides the pedestrian area into a public promenade bounded by two entry courts on the east and west that will each include a neoclassical guardhouse and bollards to block most vehicular traffic. The entry courts feature large a grid of granite pavers in varying shades of gray. Eighty-eight elm trees are to be planted within the area, offering shade and providing a more human scale to the long expanse.

Acute political and practical sensitivities led to alterations in the final design. Compromises were also driven by concerns about maintenance during winter, accessibility for official vehicles, and a desire to make the design removable should Pennsylvania Avenue revert back to a public roadway.

For example, the fine gravel-like paving specified for the promenade area was changed to a brown-tinted aggregate that will be easier to maintain during winter. A proposed lane bounded by an allee of trees along the northern sidewalk of the promenade was to accommodate a bus route and reduce the large scale of the wide promenade area. However, planting the trees caused concern that it would be practically and politically difficult to reopen Pennsylvania Avenue as a public road at some time in the future. Therefore, planting the allee has been put aside for now.

There are many examples of urban streetscapes throughout this country that have been designed to create delightful pedestrian experiences. A complexity of site elements is woven together to create a coherent order to the urban street. These designs provide horizontal and vertical spatial definitions that give these streets a human scale. They provide an attractive enticement for

Trees, clock, lightpoles, bike racks and the incorporation of sculptural elements enrich the pedestrian experience. Security design implementations should adhere to the same design principles we would apply to any site design project.

A streetscape with some "hardening" of the site elements, could provide a high level of perimeter security.

The site elements that can be used to protect public gathering spaces can be a positive expression of the special nature of the building and its function. A good example is this water-wall with bollards at The Salt Lake Palace Convention Center designed by Thompson, Ventulett, Stainback + Associates, that punctuates the end of the street at this entrance to the exhibition hall.

pedestrians that bring all the positive attributes that their presence inherently delivers to a downtown. These pedestrian spaces were not necessarily designed to address the perimeter security requirements that have become so much a part of today's urban streetscapes. But it is not difficult to imagine that with minor modifications and element "hardening" these streetscapes could be responsive in addressing today's need for perimeter security design.

This "participatory" fountain design by Sasaki Associates as part of their plan for the Charleston Waterfront Park in South Carolina, celebrates this entry to a major public space. Although not the original design objective, this fountain along with a change in elevation, creates a formidable vehicular barrier. There's no reason that security design requirements should steer us away from achieving design excellence in our site design responses.

As landscape architects, we know how to design places that make people want to use them. We know how to create "a sense of place" and complement an area's identity. The site elements and amenities that we use to create these perceptual qualities of place and identity must continue to be the foundation on which we build our security designs. Along with our other design considerations, security design must be integrated holistically and seamlessly into a comprehensive site design approach.

# Index

Access control, 25, 44, 70–72, 131–134. *See also* Guards; Perimeter security
ASIS, *see* Security consultants

Background checks for frequent visitors, 163
Balancing security and openness, 2, 7–9, 20, 131, 167, 171–172, 178–179
Barriers, *see* Hardened; Perimeter security; Street Furnishings
  beam barriers, 47, 50, 52–53, 170
  bollards, 12–13, 17, 47, 55– 61, 68, 84–99, 101, 103–105, 109, 112–114, 121, 123–124, 137–140, 142, 148, 152–155, 158–159, 162, 170, 172
  collapsible, removable, and retractable, 57–58, 84, 95, 98–99, 105, 113–114, 137–138, 170
  footings, 59, 68. *See also* Hardened
  minimum height, number, and spacing, 55, 58
  cantilever and truck gates, 52
  footings, *see* Hardened
  rising vehicular barriers, 50–51, 54, 131, 133, 170
  tensioned steel cables, 159
Benches, *see* Street furnishings
Bike racks, *see* Street furnishings

Bollards, *see* Barriers; Street furnishings
Bombs:
  car bombs, 30–31, 44, 50, 170
  effects of bomb blasts, 28–29, 44
"Bunker Pots," *see* Street furnishings

Collaboration between professions, 3, 17, 161–167
Complementing existing architecture, 15–16, 48–50, 54–55, 57, 61–62, 64, 75, 83–160, 170, 172, 174
Concepts of site security design, 33–76. *See also* Perimeter Security
  access control, see Access control
  barriers, *see* Barriers
  designing to performance standards, 33, 74–75
  designing to the threat level, 33, 74–75
  layered perimeter, 44, 71–72, 162–163
  risk, *see* Publications; Risk
  setbacks, *see* Perimeter security; Setbacks
  site survey, 33–34
  threat analysis, *see* Threats
  visual surveillance, see Guards; Visual surveillance
Cost of enhanced security, 15–17, 21

**191**